BUILDING FINANCIAL HABITS

A TEENAGER'S QUICKSTART TO FINANCIAL LITERACY

F. C. RAMIREZ

© **Copyright 2022 - All rights reserved.**

The content contained within this book may not be reproduced, duplicated or transmitted without direct written permission from the author or the publisher.

Under no circumstances will any blame or legal responsibility be held against the publisher, or author, for any damages, reparation, or monetary loss due to the information contained within this book, either directly or indirectly.

Legal Notice:

This book is copyright protected. It is only for personal use. You cannot amend, distribute, sell, use, quote or paraphrase any part, or the content within this book, without the consent of the author or publisher.

Disclaimer Notice:

Please note the information contained within this document is for educational and entertainment purposes only. All effort has been executed to present accurate, up to date, reliable, complete information. No warranties of any kind are declared or implied. Readers acknowledge that the author is not engaged in the rendering of legal, financial, medical or professional advice. The content within this book has been derived from various sources. Please consult a licensed professional before attempting any techniques outlined in this book.

By reading this document, the reader agrees that under no circumstances is the author responsible for any losses, direct or indirect, that are incurred as a result of the use of the information contained within this document, including, but not limited to, errors, omissions, or inaccuracies.

CONTENTS

Introduction	5
1. BRING ON THE MONEY	11
The Financial Overview	12
Personal Finance—Could It Be for Younger People?	14
Why Learn Personal Finance at an Early Age	15
The Future of Teen Finance	18
The Stories of Teen Finance	25
2. EARLY AGE BANKING	29
The Bank Account: An Overview	30
What Can You Do With a Bank Account?	34
What are the Best Banks Available for Teens?	38
The Steps to Opening an Account	41
The Eligibility Questionnaire	43
The Goal Questionnaire	44
3. LET'S FILL THAT BANK ACCOUNT	47
The Income Overview	48
Common Jobs That Teens Currently Do	53
Finding Your Skills	56
What Skills Do You Need for Your First Job?	58
The Creative Ways to Earn an Income for Teens	62
Steps to Applying for Jobs	65
The Mock Interview	68
The Millionaire Habits	69
4. HANDLING YOUR EXPENSES	71
Budgeting: The Overview	71
Wants Versus Needs	73
The Budget Practice	75
Strategies for Budgeting	79

The Millionaire Habits	84
The Bottom Line	85

5. **THE SECRETS OF THE CREDIT CARD** — 89
   - Credit Cards: The Overview — 90
   - What Teens Can Do With a Credit Card — 92
   - The Ins and Outs of a Credit Score — 94
   - Getting a Credit Card — 96
   - Lessons to Learn With Credit Cards — 98
   - Choosing a Credit Card — 101
   - Millionaire Habits — 101

6. **SHAPE YOUR FUTURE AND INVEST** — 103
   - The Investing Overview — 104
   - The Basics of Investing — 106
   - Types of Investments — 110
   - Investing Skills for Teenagers — 114
   - The Golden Rules of Investing — 117
   - Best Applications for Investing — 119
   - Creating a Mock Portfolio — 125
   - Millionaire Habits — 126

7. **HERE COMES THE FUTURE** — 129
   - The Retirement Overview — 130
   - Reasons Why Teenagers Should Start Saving for Retirement — 131
   - Planning for Retirement — 132
   - Examples of Teenagers Who Are Planning For Retirement — 135
   - Steps to Plan for Retirement — 136
   - The Retirement Calculator — 139

8. **THE TEENAGE FINANCE GLOSSARY** — 141
   - The Finance Glossary for Teens — 142

Conclusion — 157
References — 161

INTRODUCTION

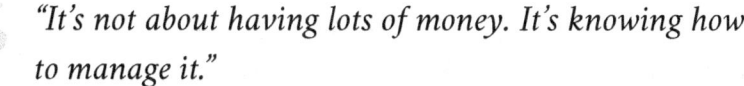 *"It's not about having lots of money. It's knowing how to manage it."*

— UNKNOWN

Have you ever heard about a 10-year-old girl who made her way from decorating lockers to becoming a teenage millionaire? Maybe not, but we are talking about Maddie Bradshaw! The then 10-year-old went to the shops with the hope of finding something that she could use to decorate her school locker but couldn't find what matched her desires. As young as she was, she saw a market gap because no company was able to provide her with what she wanted. Bradshaw was keen to find a solution and her dream came true when her uncle gave her a non-operational coke machine, alongside 50 bottle caps, as a gift. The little girl put her creative abilities into play and made 50 pieces of art from the bottle caps.

Bradshaw then put magnets inside the bottle caps so that they could stick on metal lockers, thereby creating unique decorations that caught the eyes of other children in her class. In no time, the magnetized caps were trending in the whole school. At the age of 12, Maddie started growing her cap business idea with the help of her mother. She only had a few hundred dollars, which she invested into creating jewelry using bottle caps. Her brand included necklaces that had exchangeable accessories, magnetic pendants, and "Snap Caps," which were fun pieces of jewelry.

Maddie kept on working on new designs for bottle caps together with her sister. When she was only 13, she made her first million from a bottle cap idea! Maddie did not stop there. She went on to pitch her business on Shark Tank, where a panel of investors will be available to put in their money for lucrative and promising business ideas. Already this shows that the teenager's mindset was now oriented toward explosive business and financial growth. Fortunately, Maddie's Snap Caps won the heart of three investors, and this accelerated her growth even more. Now, do you see that being a teenager does not stop you from showcasing entrepreneurial thinking? You can even make and manage your own money, just like Bradshaw, who found her way to financial independence through bottle caps!

You don't need to wait until you are older before you start thinking about money and coming up with investing strategies. When you start earning money through your own hard work, you will progressively learn to value every cent. You become more careful in making sure that the way you use your money aligns with your goals and priorities. Besides, it feels good to be financially independent without burdening your parents. If your parents are going through a hard time financially, you make things easier for them when you make and manage your own money.

As they say, "The journey of a thousand miles begins with one step." You need to start thinking about your future now. Also, it's important to know that walking a thousand miles is a time-related effort. The earlier you start the journey, the greater the likelihood of getting to the destination earlier. This means that if you intend to enjoy money and possibly retire early, consider learning various aspects of money now, including budgeting, saving, expenditure, and investing strategies. You wouldn't want to be part of the "rat race" until you are old, do you? If not, then this book is a relevant tool that will assist you to grow expertise in handling finances from your teenage years.

Do you sometimes feel so lost in the direction your life should take? You are not sure of whether it's best to get a job, invest, or simply enjoy your childhood and worry about money later. Could it be that your teenage years would have been more exciting if you had enough money to fund your desires? You don't want to ask your parents for money for virtually everything, even their birthday gifts. You might be tired of having to save for months or even years before you can afford a road trip. If any of these sentiments describe what you are going through, please take note that there are many more teenagers out there who are having the same experiences. The better part is that this book was written with you in mind so that you can break free from the "financial dependency" trap.

You might be one of those who blame themselves for a birth timing that caused you to spend your teenage years during an era that is characterized by economic crises and global pandemics. Jobs are generally scarce, and realizing your dreams seems more difficult than ever. As a result, you might feel like you are caught up in the "There are no jobs anyways, so who cares?" syndrome. Anxiety and frustration have been the order of each day, but not after reading through this financial guide that has been custom-made for you and your agemates. This book will assist you in building habits that will enhance financial literacy and defy all odds that hinder you from making it.

Be prepared to get the following benefits from reading this book:

- financial literacy
- how to invest
- how to save money

- how to plan for retirement

Welcome to the road to teenage financial independence! This "must-have" guide will help you to maneuver through money-related aspects like budgeting and saving. By the time you get to the end of this book, you will become more confident in handling your finances and approaching your future. The information that is provided in this book will assist you in easily seeing opportunities for making money, which is a vital step toward financial independence. This book will develop or boost your optimism so that you see a bright future ahead of you and work toward making it a reality. Happy financial independence.

1

BRING ON THE MONEY

Imagine how much money you would be having by now if you had decided to save just 10% of your pocket money or any other funds that you got. You would probably have accumulated enough capital for a business venture that would take you to your next financial status. This piece of information might get you wondering, "But I still need to party, shop, and go out with friends." The good news is that you can still have fun and save at the same time. All you need is to learn how to do this well and develop financial discipline. You won't need to stress yourself about how you can budget, save, and enjoy your life because this chapter will guide you. Not only that, but this chapter will also introduce you to the world of personal finance. You will also be further enlightened on the reasons why financial literacy is of paramount importance.

THE FINANCIAL OVERVIEW

Is there any difference between the words "money" and "finance?" Yes, there is. Money could refer to the currency that you give or get in exchange for something. You buy your candy with money, not finance. However, money is a vital part of finance. We cannot talk about finances without talking about money. Finance is a broader word that involves various aspects of money, including how to acquire, use, and generally manage it. With this understanding in mind, let's go through a general overview of what finance involves.

Personal Finance

The phrase "personal finance" is used to describe all activities and procedures for managing your money. This includes saving, spending, generating income, and protecting your money. Let's have a quick look at some of the terms that you should know as far as personal finance is concerned.

Income

This refers to the money that you receive and is commonly known as cash inflow. You may have different sources of income. If your parents regularly give you some pocket money, that is also a source of income. If you do something for the lady next door in exchange for money, that's another income source. The more income you get, the more money you may have in your reserves at any given time.

Spending

The way you use the money that you receive is known as spending. The things that you spend your money on are what we call expenses. You can spend your money on services such as getting your favorite shoe fixed. You can also spend on goods like food. It is also important for you to know that any spending that you do is categorized into two classes, that is, cash and credit. Cash spending is when you use the money that you have at hand to purchase something. In credit spending, you use borrowed money to make your payments. Please note that each time you spend money, the amount that you have reduces. This means that the more you spend, the lesser money you will still have available in your reserves. Therefore you need to be careful about how you spend your money.

Saving

Saving involves setting aside some money for future use. Normally, you save your surplus so that your everyday needs are still met. This makes it easier for you not to think of using the money that you would have saved. The surplus is the money that remains after you have subtracted your spending from your income. The ability to fund and manage a savings account is a crucial part of personal finance. This area could determine the rate at which you grow financially.

People who do not save have little to no chances of growing their money because they use every cent that comes their way. You wouldn't want to fall in that category, would you? Well, how you spend your money greatly determines how much you can possibly save. This means that you can increase your savings by reducing unnecessary spending and proper planning.

Investing

Investing is the art of purchasing certain assets with the hope that they will increase in value so that you can get more money than you invested. Simply put, it is a strategy for growing your money, though this comes with a lot of risks that can see you losing all your money. Though this area is much dominated by individuals who are over the age of 18, young teenagers can invest under the surveillance of their parents. Investing is one of the areas that may require advice from financial professionals to ensure that you do it right.

PERSONAL FINANCE—COULD IT BE FOR YOUNGER PEOPLE?

Personal finance is important for younger people, especially teenagers, more than you can ever imagine. Available information reveals that the majority of experts believe that, by the time a child reaches the age of eight, their basic math is good enough for them to start learning about money. If they are taught about finances at this age, they grasp the concepts quite well. What more would a teenager do? Teenagers who master the ideas of creating income, saving, and spending at an early age are more likely to be excellent at managing their finances as adults. Therefore, getting better at personal finance during your teenage years lays a foundation for better financial security as you grow.

WHY LEARN PERSONAL FINANCE AT AN EARLY AGE

Building incredible financial habits is as important to teenagers as it is to adults. This means that as a teenager, there is no way you will escape having to deal with personal finance. Therefore, the earlier you start mastering the concepts of personal finance, the better. Let's explore more reasons why learning personal finance at a young age is an adventure to explore.

They Learn the Value of the Dollar

When, as a teenager, you are given the chance to oversee your own finances, you can easily learn the value of each dollar that you get. Imagine being given some money by a parent as pocket money. Seeing that money shrink as you tap your card to buy things can open your eyes to the world of financial realities. Just the idea of knowing what a dollar can buy and how you can lose it in a moment helps to instill financial values in you. This is different when you simply ask your parents to tap their card to buy everything that you feel you deserve.

To Make Saving One of Their Healthy Habits

Saving is an act of knowing how to spend your money. Spending is generally easy, but doing it appropriately is a challenge for many people, even adults. Studies have shown that ages between six and twelve mark the period during which many children learn and reinforce their financial values (Karr, 2022). However, the earlier you learn about aspects such as saving, the longer the timeframe during which you will practice the financial tactic. As a result, saving will become a habit.

To Enhance Financial Independence

Having to depend on your parents or guardians for every debit card swipe doesn't feel so good. You can probably attest to that feeling. You feel awesome when you have the leverage to swipe your own card when you need or want something. This helps you to develop the ability to save for future dates or bigger things. Suppose you save a few dollars and then impulsively spend them on pizza, then you won't be able to get what you have been saving for. While this might seem like a painful process, it actually trains you to be more responsible for what happens to your money. You learn to uphold financial principles. If you again try to save for something and you succeed in buying it, you will certainly love the feeling.

They Learn How to Stay Out of Debt in the Future

One of the truths that you should know is that you will not be able to afford everything that you need there and then. For you to then get such things, it's either you save and buy later, or you use credit and buy immediately. The first option requires financial literacy and self-control, while the second one needs less of that. Therefore, if you learn financial literacy at a younger age, the likelihood of staying out of debt is relatively higher because you will be better able to save for your needs and wants.

To Grasp Financial Concepts That School Won't Teach Them

Learning personal finance at a young age allows you to put the things that you learn at school into practice. In most cases, when things are practically done, that's when you will begin to see what the theory actually means. You even get to learn some aspects that you might not have been taught in school. This is when the saying, "Experience is the best teacher," begins to work for you. For example, learning about compound interest might be very difficult to understand in theory. However, when you save your money in a tax-free savings account and you start to earn interest, everything begins to make better sense.

THE FUTURE OF TEEN FINANCE

If you have been asking, "What's in it for me?" your question will be answered in this section. We will look at what you stand to gain in the future if you invest in gaining financial literacy today. However, we cannot talk about the future of teen finance while giving a blind eye to the challenges that the young ones are currently facing. For this reason, we will kickstart this section by exploring the difficulties that teenagers are going through in relation to handling finances.

Challenges of Financing for Teens

The main challenge that comes with depending on your parents for all your financial needs will become more apparent as you grow older. Imagine that time when you will be done with college, you get a job, and you are expected to manage your money on your own. Such a scenario wouldn't be an issue for someone who learned how to manage their finances during their teenage years. We have just described a projected problem that will result if, as a teenager, you don't gain the practical experience of handling money. This projected challenge is fueled by other hurdles that we will discuss in this section.

Being Financially Literate

Properly handling finances is not an innate skill that you are born with, like your talents. It's something that you can learn and master over time. The problem is that most schools do not teach their students the nitty-gritty of financial literacy. The teenagers who tend to exhibit remarkable financial literacy are those who take the initiative to educate themselves using online tools and other resources that are accessible to them. Truth be told, if you can only find one good resource that you follow, you will have gained the basics of managing your money. You are even better positioned because you have this comprehensive guide in your possession so you will get everything that you need to know.

Repaying Education-Related Debts

Many teenagers feel pressured to attend expensive private schools in a bid to increase their chances of landing a better job when they are done. Interestingly, Shane Fischer of Winter Park, Florida, once said, "If I knew then what I know now, I wouldn't have gone to an expensive private school and would have opted for the less prestigious public school" (Fontinelle, 2022). Fischer had a point in saying so because many teenagers end up getting student loans to fund their education, but later realize that even if they get a better job, that loan cannot repay itself. Statistical reports from FinAid highlighted that 88.6% of all law students complete their education by borrowing. By the time they finish their education, their debt would be worth $80,000. This is just a speck of the number of debts that many young people find themselves in as they try to create a better future for themselves.

Learning How to Invest

Some events that affected the whole world, like the Great Recession, made current teenagers have a different look at financial aspects such as investing. This is because some of them witnessed how their parents and relatives lost a lot of money during these global downturns. The situation was even worsened by the increasing scarcity of jobs, a scenario that makes earning money quite difficult. However, it is important for you to remember that the stock market has seen many people earning great returns over the years. If you consider investing earlier, the probability of earning more in some years to come is high. Do away with the fears and invest so that you build the wealth that you will enjoy later.

Gaining the Confidence to Take Risks

Many endeavors for making money require some level of risk tolerance. Some, like investing, may involve high risks, so your tolerance should be relatively higher. Brian Ullman, who is a wealth manager at Ford Financial Group, highlighted that their younger investors exhibit low-risk tolerance attributes (Fontinelle, 2022). This is because they are more conservative in the way they handle their portfolios. According to Ullman, this might cause youngsters to lose vital opportunities for making money in the future. Such conservational positioning is something that you might have to deal with for the sake of a better future.

How to Control Your Spending

With the amount of peer pressure that you might experience out there, spending recklessly can be quite inevitable. Teenagers tend to use a lot of money on clothes, food, and other lifestyle-related forms of spending. When you learn to live within your own means, you may become more responsible in your spending. The focus is not much on earning more but on spending less. When you master the concept of reducing your spending, then you will have more to save and invest.

Knowing What You Want in the Future

One of the major issues that teenagers face is that they might not even know what they want for their future. Who do you want to be five, ten, twenty, or forty years from now? What kind of lifestyle would you want to lead together with your future family? When do you intend to retire? Giving sincere answers to such questions gives you an idea of the future that you look forward to. Such knowledge influences the way you handle your finances now as you head into the future.

Zooming Into the Future of a Literate Teen

A teenager who is literate when it comes to finances has a different way of handling finances compared to their friends. There is a certain shift in the mindset that they attain and they keep getting better every day. This section is dedicated to discussing the perceptions and actions of a financially literate teen around money. As you read through this section, visualize yourself being that teen who would have benefited from this literacy. In other words, this section describes the financially literate version of yourself.

You Can Prioritize Needs Over Wants

When you become financially literate, you will be able to distinguish between a need and a want. Basically, a need is a necessity that you cannot do without, while a want is some form of luxury. So, if you don't have a smartphone, this might be a need because you probably want to use it for research and communication. However, pushing for the latest smartphone is no longer within the needs limits. It's a want. Driving to school isn't really a need because you can still do so, even without it. Please note that this does not mean that your wants are completely irrelevant. You can still cater to your wants, but after you have allocated enough funds for your needs and saved some money for emergencies. Simply put, the issue of needs and wants is a matter of prioritization, to ensure that you don't fail to pay your rent after spending all your money on video games.

You Can Budget Clearly and Professionally

Financial literacy trains you to track your spending so that you can put together a realistic budget that supports your growth. Creating a budget will assist you to devise other indirect savings strategies that you might have never considered. For example, if you track your spending and notice that there are some paid apps that you are using, you can easily switch to the free ones, thereby saving in the process.

For budgeting, you can employ free money management apps like Every Dollar and Wally. The budget won't need to be complicated. However, be sure to include spending, saving, and giving. The budget will help you to spend responsibly despite the fact that you will be seeing a lot of money in the bank. When you come across reasonable causes for giving, you won't need to worry about digging into your savings pocket because of the "giving fund" that you set aside when you made your budget.

You Can Accumulate a Good Chunk of Savings for Emergencies

It's easier for you to track your current spending habits when you are financially literate. This gives you room to make adjustments to your budget as necessary. You begin to work toward spending less than what you earn, thereby accumulating more savings over time. As time progresses, you should aim for growing the gap between your spending and earnings, which gives you more leverage to save. Understanding finances enlightens you to the fact that there is no growth when you spend every dollar that you get.

Utilizing the Power of a Credit Score

When you understand various concepts around money, you can't afford to jeopardize your credit score for anything, that is if you have a credit card. You will understand how important it is to maintain a good credit score so you will do your best to avoid keeping high balances in your account, as well as making late or minimal payments. Otherwise, you might end up failing to pay off your debt, thereby negatively affecting your credit score.

You might be wondering why credit scores are that crucial. They come in handy when you need to save money on utilities. If you decide to get an apartment, a high credit score elevates the probability of getting good deals for rental and loan agreements. Financially literate people are better protected from credit card scams because they check to see if no one else opened a credit card using their name. Otherwise, if that happens, their credit score may be negatively impacted because the scammers are more likely to display financial irresponsibility using your name. Also, you should be careful of sites that ask you to pay money for you to access your credit report. Each of the three credit bureaus that exist allow you to get a free copy of your credit score report once every year.

Understand How the World Works in Terms of Money

Money is the currency that keeps the world running. For you to get something, you will need money to buy it. That means that you should also devise strategies for earning money. You could sell some goods or services to accumulate funds. As we mentioned earlier, keeping your expenditure lower than your earnings is a worthwhile skill.

THE STORIES OF TEEN FINANCE

It might not be that surprising to come across individuals who made it in the world of finance while they were in their twenties. The case becomes remarkably unique when teenagers own companies as well as excel in making and managing money. This section will give you interesting examples of such teens who defied all odds in the finance world. You could be one of them if you learn from their stories and get inspired.

Mikayla Ulmer

Mikayla Ulmer is the creator of the Me & the Bees lemonade brand, which they made when they were only 13 years of age. Amazing, right? Even more interestingly, by the time Mikayla had reached the age of nine (quite young), they had sold lemonade that was worth $11 million. This continued to inspire them until the Me & the Bees lemonade brand came to life. The name "Me & the Bees" emanated from the fact that Mikayla was stung by a bee and survived the incident.

Striking a deal with Whole Foods Market saw Mikayla's business grow even bigger. At the moment, Mikayla donates some of the proceeds from their business to bee conservation endeavors. They are also demonstrating an amazing ability to balance their schoolwork and business. Mikayla is now diversifying into creating other product lines, such as the natural beeswax lip balm. You can draft a new perspective of your entrepreneurial and finance journey by deriving inspiration from this teenager!

Jeremy Miller

Business endeavors are never immune to failure, but with determination, you will eventually make it. The story of Jeremy Miller is a good example of exhibiting this fact. Miller is now 20 years old, but their entrepreneurial journey began when they were only 16. At that time, Miller created a company called Void Longboards, which eventually crumbled despite all efforts to keep it up and running. This could have demotivated Miller, but instead, they formed a new company by the name of J R Miller Group, which is a social media consultancy. There is no room for accommodating failure, and certainly, age cannot be your limitation.

Sean Belnick

Sean Belnick is the brains behind bizchair.com, and they founded this company when they were 14 years old. This company is an online retailer of any type of furniture that you can think of. Belnick didn't wait until they accumulated thousands of dollars for them to start their business. Instead, they kickstarted their business with only $500 and ran it from their bedroom at that time. Belnick then escalated their business from there. Having moved to their first 40,000-

square-foot warehouse in 2004, Belnick moved to a 702,000-square-foot warehouse within five years. Belnick's business accumulated more than $58 million in sales. As of now, the net worth of Sean Belnick is reported to be $42 million. You also have what it takes to make such earnings!

By now, you should have a better view of monetary issues as a teenager. Hopefully, you won't be distancing yourself from aspects that involve money anymore, considering that you have learned that teenagers can also take part in the financial world. In the next chapter, you will have more insights about bank accounts, ranging from how to open one and the nitty gritty of using them to manage your money. If you are also wondering why bank accounts are that important, the next chapter will enlighten you about that, too.

2

EARLY AGE BANKING

Most teens can testify that nothing compares to that feeling of financial independence. When teenagers start earning income, their sense of independence increases, and they start feeling like capable adults. However, being an adult comes with a lot of decision-making, and one of the most crucial decisions is deciding whether to bank their money or not. With the many misconceptions that exist concerning banks, most teenagers are hesitant when it comes to opening bank accounts and depositing their money. Have you ever had this experience before? It makes sense if you did because many people do not trust banks, but this is due to a lack of knowledge about banking and bank operations. The truth is, as a teen, you can actually trust banks to manage and protect your hard-earned money from unfortunate things like fires or even theft. Fortunately, this chapter will educate you about banks: what they are, how they operate, and why they are necessary. By the time you get to the end of the chapter, we trust that you will have gained more confidence to open and manage your bank account.

THE BANK ACCOUNT: AN OVERVIEW

For teens, savings and checking accounts are the most recommended ones (Forbes, 2022). A savings account is basically meant for you to save your money, so you deposit funds that will earn interest over time and grow. A checking account, on the other hand, is a bank account that you can use on a daily basis to make different transactions. For you to fully understand how banks can be beneficial to you, let us look at some of the benefits these types of accounts come with. Having a savings or checking account can help you become more independent as a teen. With emerging technological advancements, you can keep tabs on your spending habits. Being aware of how much money you spend each month will alert you to the adjustments you might need to make in order to progressively save more.

The internet has made activities like shopping a lot easier, and you are only able to shop online if you have a checking account. A checking account will also allow you to pay for anything online, for example, school fees and cell phone bills. With increased interaction with banks, your knowledge of finances will broaden. In most cases, most teenagers will be intrigued to start thinking about important things like retirement or investments and start planning a better future for themselves. With savings and checking accounts, you will benefit from services like loans, debt consolidation services, and budget guidance.

Are There Bank Accounts Specifically for Teens?

A checking account is just what a teenager needs in order to learn good spending habits because it allows them to keep track of the cash flow in the account. This is especially important if you are just starting college or going straight into the workforce. Keep in mind that it is important that a guardian is involved when you are choosing the correct type of bank account. The goal is to choose a type of account that is user-friendly for you as a teenager. It is important to look at factors like mobile banking, involved fees and monthly minimums, guardian control, and account conversions.

Since the majority of teenagers spend most of their time on their phones, it only makes sense that the best bank account for a teenager should come with mobile banking. You could be smiling at this idea right now. Being able to pay for anything using a phone only makes life easier for young adults. The bank account should also have affordable fees that come with each mobile transaction. Before opening a bank account, you and your parents should first find out about the fees and monthly minimums involved. This is important because teenagers usually have limited sources of money, though you have the leverage to grow your money. It is best for you to go for an account that has little to no fees and/or monthly minimums.

Most banks require a guardian to set withdrawal limits for their teenager's bank account. Other banks keep parents in the loop by sending them text messages to let them know what their teenager is up to with their bank account. If the bank account does not have the guardian control option, the parent can decide to be a joint account holder instead. It is a relief to know that most bank accounts will require a guardian if a teenager wants to open an account and is below 18 years of age. A parent should find out what happens to the account when the teenager reaches a certain age limit. It is important to know if there will be any changes to services or fees. We recommend that you choose an account that will come with as few changes as possible.

Do Teenagers Really Need Bank Accounts?

Have you ever been wondering, "Do I really need a bank account?" The straightforward answer is that you sure do. If you want to feel more like an adult, responsible and independent, then try opening a checking account. Just the fact that this account will be in your name will get you excited enough. To better explain why you need a bank account, let us explore the benefits a bank account will have for teenagers.

As a teenager, you are just at the doorstep of adulthood, and a bank account at a young age will teach you just the skills to manage your money as you become a full-grown adult. Aspects like mobile banking, using credit or debit accounts, and depositing or withdrawing money will not be new to you if you start dealing with them now. This will further help you not to fall prey to fraud. A bank account will also help you learn to budget well as you notice how your spending habits impact your account balances. A bank account for a teenager is just the head start they need to build their future financial history. With the help of your guardian, you will learn to shave off bad financial habits that could potentially affect your financial history in the long run.

Can Teens Open Bank Accounts on Their Own?

Teens under the age of 18 cannot open bank accounts on their own. Please note that the legal age for opening bank accounts may differ by state. This legal age determines when you can be involved in signing contracts. Some of the requirements for teens to open bank accounts include being in possession of a national ID and a certain amount of money for an opening deposit. There are, however, other options banks provide for teens who want to open accounts, even before they reach 18 years of age.

You can try opening a joint account, where one of the account holders is of legal age or older. Usually, the other account holder can be your guardian. You can also apply for a type of account that is specifically targeted toward teens who are not yet of legal age. In this case, you will also need your parent to be one of the account holders. Both accounts have full parental control, so your activities will be under surveillance. When opening these accounts, you and your parent need to know all the fee requirements so that you do not fall short or get penalized for late payments. A history of late payments will decrease your chances of other banks doing business with you. Banks will also run a criminal check on you. If you are in the United States, you will need to be a citizen of the U.S. for you to be eligible to open a bank account.

WHAT CAN YOU DO WITH A BANK ACCOUNT?

It is no secret that teens who have bank accounts are better off financially than those without them. This means that opening your bank account will put you in a better financial position as you will see in this section.

Getting Started With Saving

If you open a savings account, the bank has a certain interest rate that it will offer you. This interest will make your money grow with time. Be mindful, though, of all the fees that come with your savings account so that you don't end up paying more than you are gaining. Your bank account should come with fees that are less than the interest. If you have a checking and a savings account, both registered with the same bank, you can request for the money in your checking account to be transferred to your savings account so that it can grow over time. You can also cash checks at a bank where you have an active account for free. Someone who does not have a bank account will be charged a certain fee if they want to cash a check.

Someone without a bank account will have to rely on a credit card to get a cash advance if they need cash, which will come with fees. But if you have a bank account, you can get access to cash without a fee if you use your bank. With a bank account, you are also able to pay your bills or write checks for free, but someone without a bank account will be charged to do so.

Using a Checking Account For Your Day-to-Day Spending

Having a checking account provides you with lots of conveniences, including the ability to perform day-to-day transactions easily, even in the comfort of your home. If you do not have a bank account, you are forced to be constantly dependent on cash. You can also write checks for people instead of carrying cash around, as the latter is not safe. You also have the privilege of using ATM machines to get cash if you need it and swiping when buying goods in stores.

Learning How to Manage Money

When it comes to spending money, getting carried away happens to all of us. With a bank account, however, you have a higher chance of managing your money better than someone who does not have one. Banks have also introduced low-balance alerts. You set a certain amount as a limit for low balances. This means that when your account balance goes below that, the bank will send you an alert, usually in the form of a text, email, or just a push notification. This helps you manage your money well and also avoid overdrawing your bank account. Banks do have an option for automatic online bill payment. This is a great help if you sometimes find yourself falling behind on your bill payments. This also helps you escape situations where you find yourself running out of money before paying your bills due to bad spending habits. If you do not sign up for automatic bill payment, you can just set up your account so that you receive notifications of your upcoming bills before they are due.

Sub-accounts for savings are also an option you have if you want to manage your money wisely. Most people are so reluctant to open savings accounts if they are not saving for anything. Sub-accounts for saving are a type of savings account, but with a goal. Knowing that you are saving for something specific will motivate you to spend your money wisely. Automatic savings deposits are another option for good money management. You set a certain amount that will automatically be deposited into your savings account. This can be weekly, monthly, or even after each quarter of the year. There are also a lot of budgeting tools available on a lot of banks' websites. These tools will provide you with useful tips on how you can manage your money well.

Use a Safe Environment to Learn About the Responsibility of Money

We all want a conducive environment for keeping our money safe, and because of this, banks have created what is called financial inclusion. They have tried their best to make banks a friendly place for everyone, including teens. Some banks have held events where members are taught more about banking and how to use money responsibly. They have made financial education tools for their members online. Banks are safe, and you should feel comfortable entrusting them with your money. The more you visit your bank, the easier it is for you to create relationships with the workers that will cheer you on as you go ahead on your journey of wise money management. These people will have your best interests at heart and will not hesitate to give good advice when it comes to your money.

WHAT ARE THE BEST BANKS AVAILABLE FOR TEENS?

Opening a bank account is a step in the right direction for you as a teen. But choosing the right bank can be quite tricky. There are factors that you need to compare before you can select the right bank. Earlier in this chapter, we mentioned that checking and savings accounts are recommended for teens because they are well-suited to cater to their needs. Let us take a look at the types of checking and savings bank accounts that you can consider choosing from.

Checking Account

A checking account is a type of bank account that you can use for daily transactions like paying your bills or buying your groceries. Here are some examples of checking accounts that are available for you as a teen.

Axos Bank First Checking

Axos Bank First Checking scores first place when it comes to banks that are user-friendly for teens. You can open an account with this bank at the age of 13. The minimum deposit is $50, and there are no fees involved after that. This bank allows your money to earn interest, and it is available online. The disadvantages, though, are that it does not allow cash deposits and it has no financial education tools.

Capital One Money

Capital One Money Bank does not require you to pay a minimum deposit before you open an account. You just have to be eight years old to be eligible to open an account with this bank. If you open an account with this bank, you will have access to online budgeting tools and ATM withdrawals that do not come with fees. However, this bank doesn't provide the much-needed customer service. It also lacks the bill payment option.

Alliant Credit Union Teen Checking

Alliant Credit Union Teen Checking does not come with a minimum deposit, but it comes with a $25 NSF fee. You should be 13 years of age to apply for an account. This bank does not have a monthly service maintenance fee. The challenge could be the fact that you have to be a member of a credit union.

Copper

Copper Bank does not have a minimum deposit, and no fees are involved, except for instances when you use an ATM from a different bank. You must be at least 13 years of age to open an account with Copper Bank. This bank provides you with financial education tools and a savings feature. The only problem is that it does not offer interest, and its parental control is not quite clear.

Connexus Credit Union

Connexus Credit Union has no minimum deposit, fees, or monthly service fees. It offers tools that will help you avoid overdrafts. It has full parental control, but your parent is required to have an active Connexus Credit Union account.

Chase First Banking

Chase First Banking does not come with a minimum deposit. It does have a fee of $2.50 if you use another bank's ATM to withdraw money. The minimum age limit is six years of age, which is the lowest age limit when compared to other banks. This bank allows full parental control. The challenges are that your parent is required to have an active Chase account. Please note that this bank does not offer interest.

Savings Accounts

A savings account is a type of account that is solely used for saving. Due to this, it has a limited amount and number of withdrawals. Let us go over the available savings account options that are at your disposal.

Alliant Credit Union Kids Savings Account

Alliant Credit Union Kids Savings Account does not have a monthly maintenance fee or a minimum deposit. It has an interest yield of up to 1.70% per year. For you to qualify, you should be 12 years of age or younger. Your guardian has to be a member of the credit union in order to have access to your account.

BECU Early Saver

BECU Early Saver has no minimum deposit or monthly maintenance fee. You can earn up to 4.70% interest each year. It is possible for your guardians to form a joint account with you, but only if they also have an active BECU account.

Bethpage Young Adult

Bethpage Young Adult Banking has a minimum deposit of $5 and a monthly maintenance fee. With this bank, you can earn up to 3.00% interest every year. Account holders should be aged between 18 and 20, and they have full control of their accounts.

Capital One Kids Savings Account

The Capital One Kids Savings Account has no monthly fees or a minimum deposit. You can yield up to 0.3% interest per year. This bank account is accessible online, and it has full parental control.

THE STEPS TO OPENING AN ACCOUNT

As you become an adult, you are going to discover that you will be required to make a lot of decisions, and before making them, you need to look at the requirements, advantages, and disadvantages. The same goes for opening an account; there are a lot of factors you should also take into consideration. Let us dive deeper into the steps you are required to take in order to open an account.

Step 1: Choose Your Bank

You need to compare the different terms and conditions of different banks so that you can choose a bank that will cater to all your needs and wants. For example, having access to an ATM, being able to pay your bills online, and saving. In choosing the bank to work with, please consider the goal questionnaire at the end of this chapter.

Step 2: Gather the Documents Needed by the Bank

These documents include your national ID or birth certificate, as well as your guardian's identity documents. You can use your passport or driver's license as identification documents. You might also be required to provide proof of employment and proof of residence.

Step 3: Bring an Adult With You if You Are Under 18 Years of Age

You might be required to sign a contract, so your guardian will have to open a joint account with you and sign the contract instead.

Step 4: Fill Out the Forms at the Bank

This part involves basically taking information from your documents and transferring it onto the bank forms before submitting them.

Step 5: Provide Your Identification

Your identification documents, as well as your guardian's, will have to be photocopied, certified, and submitted. In some instances, the bank will require you to submit original copies, which you will eventually get back. Note that your driver's license or passport can also be submitted as identity documents.

Step 6: Deposit a Small Amount to Get You Started

Different banks will have varying minimum deposit fees. You might not need to deposit this minimum deposit with some banks.

THE ELIGIBILITY QUESTIONNAIRE

At the beginning of any process, there are questions you need to ask yourself beforehand to determine if you have any chance of succeeding. Every bank has certain requirements that you need to meet before you can open an account. Below are some questions you need to ask yourself before you can decide if you qualify to open a bank account.

1. Am I of legal age?
2. If required, will my guardian help me open an account?
3. Will I be able to pay the required minimum deposit?
4. Do I need to be a citizen of the country before I can open a bank account?
5. If asked, can I provide proof of payment or proof of residence?

THE GOAL QUESTIONNAIRE

Due to a lack of knowledge, many teens get into trouble when they try to open bank accounts because they do not know which bank or which type of account to choose. This section comes with a questionnaire with questions that will help you make these decisions wisely.

1. Does this bank have a minimum deposit and monthly fees?
2. Can I use an ATM for free?
3. Can I pay my bills online?
4. Does this account offer interest?
5. Will money transfers come with a fee?
6. Is there a branch near me?
7. What are the penalties for overdrafts?

8. Do I have to always keep a certain amount of money in the account?
9. Can I get access to my money online?
10. Do I have to pay to replace my card or to cash checks?

After going through this chapter, you now know why opening a bank account at a young age is of utmost importance. You are now aware of the various banks and bank accounts available to you. Moving on to the next chapter, you are going to be educated on how you can make money and be able to fill the bank account that you will create.

3

LET'S FILL THAT BANK ACCOUNT

> "Financial freedom is freedom from fear."
>
> — ROBERT T. KIYOSAKI

Most parents and guardians have it in mind that the reason why they raise their kids is to prepare them for their lives out in the real world. Families have their own set of values they pass on to their children. For instance, a family can value respect, empathy, kindness, and more. In defiance of the moral or the ethical code of your family, almost all caregivers and parents struggle to find a work ethic for their children. However, everyone should work on earth for a living. This is why we encourage guardians to teach you, children, how to work so that you will be ready for whatever life has to offer you. We also recommend you, as a teen, to observe the work ethic of your guardians, elders, and other people that you can admire in the world so that you develop your own work ethic. This chapter will highlight some of the best strategies that you can employ to make money at your age. We will also explain some of the reasons why income is very important, even at your age.

THE INCOME OVERVIEW

Income is the money that you earn for providing a service or in exchange for distributing a product. Income is used to cover day-to-day expenses in addition to funding your investments. The common types of income may include commissions, salaries, and revenue from self-employment, just to mention a few. Pensions, social security, and stock option plans are other types of income. However, these are the types of income you earn when you retire, not now that you are still a teenager.

Is Teen Employment Pretty Common?

As a teen, you should work to obtain professional experience and save up for college. However, teen employment is not pretty common. Recent studies show that less than 30% of teenagers had their own jobs in 2020 (Kolmar, 2022). However, from 2000 to 2020, most teens lost their jobs, making teenage workers drop from 43% to 28% (Kolmar, 2022). This shows that teen employment has significantly decreased. Nowadays, you can see teens are working mostly in the retail or food industry as cashiers and cooks. However, the bottom line is that it is now difficult to find a teen job easily, but it is not impossible.

The Pros and Cons of Teens Having a Job

As you get older, your portfolio of responsibilities tends to increase. It is good for you to start working and earn your own money. Teenagers are different, and their responses to a scenario where they are now working also vary. We encourage parents to guide their children to ensure that their jobs do not interfere with other important aspects of their lives, such as academic performance. Let us look at some of the pros and cons of a teen having a job.

✛ Pros of Allowing a Teenager to Work

A job will allow teenagers to earn money. Having your own money as a teenager will offer you a tangible reward for your efforts. Through earning and spending, you will learn vital techniques in money management. You will also feel independent and empowered. Part-time jobs play an important role in transforming teens into making their own money and knowing how to manage it properly.

You will learn important skills from working. Teens who start to work while at school learn good time-management skills and organization. You also learn how to communicate and engage with colleagues and superiors, a skill that aids teamwork. Additionally, you develop a work history that will help you if you consider proceeding with the line of service or business in your adult working world.

A job will also improve your character as a teenager. Work enables you to become responsible and accountable in getting assigned tasks done. Through working, you learn how to keep commitments and operate independently. If you work less than 15 hours a week, there is a high probability that you will get better grades compared to those teens that do not work at all (James, 2020). On another note, having a job will assist you in transforming from youth to adulthood.

− Cons of Allowing a Teenager to Work

Sometimes, working makes it difficult to balance work and school. It is not easy for you as a teen to recognize how much time work can take up. However, it depends on the type of job you choose, but in most situations, you may be affected because you may put more hours into your work. This may be worse if you fail to create a reasonable schedule for completing different tasks, including studying, sports, and leisure. If you want to do everything, time might prove to be an enemy as you won't be able to do everything.

As a teen, you have a lot of events that take place in your life, like parties, competitions, games, and promotions. A job might mean missing out on a lot of such fun. In some cases, you might end up not being very efficient on your job as you try to create time for the events. So, poor planning can mess up your work and lifestyle. With good planning, you can still accommodate both work and fun. The same applies to your hobbies. Failure to strike a balance may cause more harm than good.

In most scenarios, you will find out that you cannot balance your work and your hobbies as a teen. A job may come with some stress in your life due to the responsibility that it comes with. You may even get exposed to people and situations that you might not be ready for. Also, you have less surveillance from your parents when you are at work. This makes it easy for you to fall prey to a bad company that might corrupt your character and behavior. For example, you might then get exposed to substance abuse.

If you work more than 15 hours a week, you are more likely to obtain lower grades in school compared to those students who do not work (James, 2020). If you start working as a teenager, you may start to think that childhood is ending soon, so you might end up disregarding elderly advice and control.

Why Are Jobs Important for Anyone?

It is no secret that some people hate their jobs. This could be because of bad bosses or colleagues. For others, it could be due to the lack of work-life balance. Regardless of all your reasons, you should know that having a job brings many benefits to your life. It will allow you to live comfortably and add stability to you and your loved ones. Having a job can assist you in building the skills and experience you will use in the future. Let's highlight a couple of the benefits of having a job in this section.

- **You earn money:** One of the most important benefits of being employed is that you will get money. In general, we all need money to cover our expenses.
- **You get recognition:** Suppose someone asks you, "John, what do you do for a living?" This is one of the most difficult questions to answer when you are not employed, not when you are working. There is some level of confidence that comes with having a job. In other words, having a job improves your recognition and adds to your identity, making you more acceptable to your community and loved ones.
- **You continuously learn:** Another vital part of having a job is that you keep learning and constantly updating the skills you will use in the future to obtain your goals. In some situations, if you find a job in an organization, you are given all tools and resources that assist you in performing well and increasing the company's revenues. The organization will use its money and resources to teach you how to work with the tools. In simple words, it means you will be learning new things at someone else's expense, with no need to know who.

- **You gain experience:** A job will assist you in gaining practical knowledge in a specific area of the field you are interested in. It will allow you to assess whether you should pursue the same line of work or rather find different avenues in the future. When you are working in an organization, you will meet new people and create new friends who may be beneficial for you on professional, personal, and emotional fronts. Meeting new people and creating relations with them may give rise to new opportunities.
- **Other benefits:** If you are working in an office, for instance, you communicate, interact, and lead people. Doing that will improve your marketing and expand your horizons. Having a job also boosts your communication style in addition to your leadership skills. The other benefit of being employed is that you will have chances to visit new places through training, business, and conferences.

COMMON JOBS THAT TEENS CURRENTLY DO

As a teen, you should know your goals. For example, you can target to gain experience or to start creating a future career path. With your goals in mind, you can look for a part-time job that will assist you in achieving your goals. The other important thing is to understand the requirements or the experience needed for the job. You should know the location, schedule, and number of hours that you will dedicate to working. Here are some of the jobs you can do:

- **Fast food or coffee shops:** Fast food or coffee shops are some of the best places where you can get your first job as a teen. These are the places where you tend to find more vacancies. On another note, you can acquire fast food experience that you can use in the future.
- **Babysitting:** A babysitter watches and takes good care of young children when their parents are away. A babysitter may also perform duties like transporting and bathing children. This job will help you with experience in working with children. The experience will assist you if you decide to be in the field of childhood education or other careers that involve working with kids. Once you become a babysitter, you can increase your chances of being hired by doing a course through the Red Cross so that you can gain more knowledge, such as first aid.
- **Retail jobs:** Stores are some of the good places where teenagers can work. Having a job in retail stores may be very important if you work in a position that aligns with your personal goals. Most retail stores favor teenagers to work for them, so they will probably hire individuals who are 16 and older. A job in a retail shop is more likely to give you

more opportunities through meeting different people.

- **Library:** You can become a library assistant. In this case, you will work with people who visit the library, assisting them in finding books as well as checking them out. You will also help the librarian in taking inventory, digitizing printed files, and shelving books. This will give you a great deal of experience in this area. Some of the knowledge that you will gain while working in the library can come in handy in other areas of life. If you enjoy working with people and being surrounded by a wealth of knowledge, this is a great place to be!
- **Internships:** Internships allow students to apply whatever they have learned at school in real-world situations. The internship will allow you to gain more skills for your future job. This is where you can turn the theoretical knowledge that you learned from school into practical experience.
- **Delivery:** Delivering meals is another easy way to make money. A delivery job is a good side hustle for you when you go on a vacation. It will provide you with quick money and some experience in doing business.

FINDING YOUR SKILLS

Job skills are used to complete your work skills. Your skills begin to matter more when you start to work. Skills can be classified into hard and soft skills. Hard skills are specifically for job knowledge you will need to perform a particular job. Soft skills are the way you respond to varying situations or how you interact with others. Finding your skills will help you to know the area you have strengths in at work.

The Skill Evaluation

There are several ways you can consider assessing skills. You can use your self-report, where your caregiver or parent can ask you several questions, and you answer them. For instance, they can ask you if you think you have the skills that you need for you to be employed. All you need is to answer honestly. These self-reports will help you to determine your performance in goal areas such as personal finance, career planning, and health. In this section, we provide you with a list of skills that are important for you to get employed. Evaluate yourself using the given options so that you can determine your areas of excellence and improvement. Use the results to work on the lagging areas to increase your chances of getting a job.

Targeted attribute	Unsatisfactory	Requires improvement	On par with expectations	Beyond expectations
Communication				
Punctuality				
Willingness to learn				
Confidence				
Professionalism				
Response to supervisor				
Quality of work				
Workplace appearance				
Knowledge of workplace				
Work attendance				
Making useful decisions				
Response to conflicts				
Cooperation with others				
Solving problems using math				

WHAT SKILLS DO YOU NEED FOR YOUR FIRST JOB?

If you want to be a competitive teenager in the job market, you should know the kind of skills that the employer is looking for. You can practice them for mastery. Having a variety of skills is good because you will probably reach your goals faster than expected. The skills that your employer may like include the following:

Communication

Most employers need employees with good communication backgrounds. Communication covers a lot of skills you need, such as public speaking, good listening, writing, and respectfully expressing ideas. You should know how to properly follow directions, attentively listen, speak in a good way so that people will understand, and ask if you need clarification.

Positive Work Ethic and Responsibility

Business employees who are motivated to fulfill their duties, check progress on their projects, be the best, and demonstrate reliability are more likely to gain the favor of potential and current employers. If you take responsibility for the tasks that you are given, you will get ahead of colleagues who do not. Employers might resent you if you are irresponsible and disorganized. For instance, habits such as coming to work late or not finishing work assignments on time are not tolerated in the industry.

Teamwork

You should be able to interact with other people and contribute to groups with effective ideas. Businesses want employees who can build good relations and contribute to the decisions within a group. You should develop a cooperative spirit so that you work with colleagues efficiently. You can learn the art of teamwork through playing sports, joining clubs, and involving yourself in group activities.

Professionalism

Many businesses want their workers to be professional. Being professional means arriving at work on time, respecting others, dressing appropriately, having a neat appearance, and using appropriate language at your workplace.

Conflict Resolution

Conflicts are inevitable when you are working with other people. You cannot avoid them. You should develop the skills to negotiate solutions to workplace and interpersonal issues. As a teenager, you are expected to know that supervisors will need people who try to understand the other individual's perspective and negotiate peacefully. Be assertive, such that you air out your views without disrespecting or hurting the dignity of others.

Problem-Solving

Employers want someone who can work on problems on their own. If you feel confident in your ability to solve problems, it means that you will not let go of opportunities. You should, ideally, critically and creatively think and contribute your ideas that lead to problem-solving. Employers want youth who are capable of using their solid reasoning to perform tasks and identify the appropriate technique that can be used at work.

Innovation is another form of problem-solving. With innovation, you make yourself an exception in this highly competitive world of business and work. Don't be afraid to come up with new thoughts and ideas. Who knows, you might be the best innovator of all time!

The skills of problem-solving are learned through practice. Your parent should allow you to deal with your problems. They should come in offering guidance, but they should at least give you space to figure out solutions on your own. It is not easy for them to watch you do that, but if you tackle a problem on your own, you build confidence to proceed to more difficult tasks.

Self-Education

Successful individuals can learn on their own. There is no school or caregiver who will teach you everything you should know. It is a good idea to ask for the information you think you do not know. However, bear in mind that some of your parents do not necessarily love being asked questions. They think you are asking too many questions, or you may ask them at a bad time when they are in the middle of something. If you have such parents, try another way you can get their attention and then ask your questions at a good time.

Flexibility

Nobody can predict the future. We see constant changes in the world, and most of them come as surprises. There will be shifts of bosses or changes of duties that can intimidate you, but promotion comes with such rolls of punches. The best way you can adapt to get prepared for the unpredictable future is to learn, adapt, and deal with any changes. If you develop the ability to flow with the changing landscape of your life, you will reduce fear and embrace new opportunities.

THE CREATIVE WAYS TO EARN AN INCOME FOR TEENS

As a teenager, you have things you need to pay for, for example, clothes, food, entertainment, and transport expenses. As you grow older, life becomes more expensive as your responsibilities increase and parents gradually reduce their direct involvement in your goals. This increases the need for you to identify various ways of earning income, some of which we will highlight in this section.

The Online Methods

If you decide that you are not an office type, you should know that there are other jobs that you can do online. Here are some of the best jobs for you.

- **Start a blog:** Blogging is a common work-from-home job that you can use to earn money online. You can blog about a topic you are interested in. For you to start, you should have an internet connection and domain names that act as options for your blog. Be sure to create regular content for your growing audience so that your business also expands.
- **Start a video-editing business:** You can choose to take videos at events or edit those that are brought by the client. You can master this art through YouTube videos and by reading about videography.

A video editing business is one of the highest-paying jobs for teens (Sarah, 2022).

- **Sell handmade crafts on Etsy:** Selling handmade crafts can be fun if you enjoy crafting. For example, you can make and sell jewelry and printables, as well as bath and body products.
- **Sell clothes online:** To sell clothes online, you can use online platforms such as Facebook, Twitter, Instagram, and YouTube to advertise your clothes and engage with customers. You can consider selling clothes as a side hustle to obtain more money each month as you commit yourself to other things.
- **Manage social media accounts:** If you know how to use social media accounts such as TikTok and Facebook, it is easy to have many followers and start getting paid for that. Some small businesses need assistance to create content and manage their social media accounts. You can identify such business gaps and use them to increase your income.

The Offline Methods

The best job for you depends on what you value. You can value a job that pays well or has a flexible schedule. You may favor the job that aligns you with your hobbies or personal interests. Whatever the case might be, you have many options at your disposal. Here are some offline jobs that you can consider:

- **Tutoring:** Some parents search for tutors to assist their children in excelling in their classes. If you have mastered a specific field, market it to your neighbors. Simply check with people in your area to see if they want a tutor for their kids. For broader interest, place some posters in town as an advertisement.
- **Lawn and landscaping services:** Landscaping is an idea that is labor-intensive and can eventually turn into a blooming business. You can do this job in your spare time. This job needs you to be creative in taking care of lawns. You can also plant garden beds, clean up after the dog, and water landscaping in the yard.
- **Pet sitting:** Pet sitting is a fun way of making money as a teen. In some situations, your employees may need you to walk their dogs. The advantage of this kind of job is that it doesn't take much time, so you also have ample time to attend to other things.
- **House sitting:** Many people need someone who can look after their houses when they are away. When you are doing house sitting, you may also be required to water plants and pick up the mail. You can start house sitting the homes of your friends. When you feel more comfortable with the job, advertise through flyers and referrals.
- **Cleaning services:** You can start by cleaning your house. Once you see you can clean houses of other people, spread the word. Your clients will provide

what you need for your operations, so it will be easier and less costly for you. You can buy your cleaning detergents and tools for a start. Advertise your work through social media or word of mouth.

- **Washing cars:** Washing cars is a great way you can adopt if you do not like yard work. You do not need more supplies for you to get started. You will need a bucket, soap, and common rags used to wash a car. You will also need a portable vacuum as well as window cleaner. To maximize your earning potential, consider meeting people at their homes or businesses.

STEPS TO APPLYING FOR JOBS

If you were struggling with how to get a job as a teen, it is vital to understand the various steps and strategies you can use to find the one that fits your goals and preferences. Let us take a quick look at the steps you should follow when applying for a job.

Determine the Type of Job You Want

You should think about the type of work you want before applying. Some of the factors you should consider may include your desired job schedule, the skills you would like to develop, and the type of environment that you prefer to work in. Once you determine the type of job you want, proceed to the next step.

Search for the Job

The next step is to search for jobs in many ways. You may check online job boards where employers put advertisements for open positions. Newspapers and other sources of information may also come in handy. You can also look on company websites and local shops that have ads on bulletin boards or windows.

Build Your Network

You should start to build your professional network. Your network may include your past or current teachers, neighbors, coaches, family, and friends. You can ask the colleagues in your network if they know of any vacancies that may be good for you to fit in. Your social network may help you look for other professional resources that are more likely to improve your skills. You will always need other people for you to become better in life.

Get a Work Permit if Needed

Applying for a permit is an added advantage if it's a requirement for you to get the job that you want. Some organizations require teenagers to have permits before employment.

Create Your Resumé

You should create a document that contains all information about your qualifications for an open job position. This is usually referred to as a resumé. This document has different sections that contain relevant information, including your past and current professional experience and skills. If you know that you do not have previous professional experience, create other sections with the reasons why you qualify for the job. You can include your hobbies, interests, accomplishments, and your native language.

Add a Cover Letter to Your Application

If it is possible, add a cover letter to your application, along with other relevant attachments such as identity documents. A cover letter is a professional document that clarifies why you are interested in that job. Together with your resumé, a well-written cover letter increases your chances of getting the job.

Submit Applications

Now, start submitting your applications for jobs. You can apply for jobs online or in person. Aim to submit at least three applications a day or more than 10 per week. This way, you increase the probability of getting responses from potential employers.

Prepare for Interviews or Job Tests

If you are among the short-listed candidates, you should attend an interview before the job. Be sure to prepare for the interview or test by researching information about the company or industry. If you receive an invitation, practice the frequently asked interview questions and get motivated.

THE MOCK INTERVIEW

Interviews require you to exhibit certain skills, such as self-confidence. You can create questions for your mock interview. The list below gives you an idea of some of the questions that can be asked in a real interview with the employer. Such questions can help you to structure your mock interview so that you can practice your answers before you get into the actual encounter with your prospective employer.

- Tell us more about yourself.
- Why did you apply for this job?
- What do you know about this company?
- What are your strengths?
- Where do you see yourself in 10 years?
- What do you think you can change in this company?
- What are your weaknesses?
- Are you able to work on weekends?
- Do you have any questions?

THE MILLIONAIRE HABITS

As you read through this book, we desire that you adopt a millionaire mindset. There are habits that are common among millionaires, and you increase your chances of being one by learning these at an early stage. In this section, we will show you some of the habits that are related to a millionaire's mindset. If there are any habits that you fall short on, work on improving and eventually mastering them.

Here are some of the millionaire habits that you should know:

- **Reading for self-improvement:** Millionaires read online books, news, and current events.
- **Creating multiple streams of income:** Millionaires do not rely on one source of income. They do that in order to handle any economic downturns, as well as to make more money.
- **Depend on monthly written budgets:** They study how much money comes in and determine what they have to do with it. In other words, they strictly follow a written budget. A budget will remove unnecessary expenses, thereby reducing the chances of overspending. Good budgets aid the achievement of set goals.
- **Avoiding debt:** They try to eliminate debt and reduce costs. They do something they know that

they should and can pay for. They live a frugal lifestyle. They always set daily goals. They use that skill to maintain focus and build their momentum. Millionaires do not act rich, and some of them are entrepreneurs.

- **Practicing patience:** A millionaire knows that patience is a virtue. They know that the key is to earn money, invest wisely, and focus on living below their means instead of searching for get-rich-quick schemes.

The next chapter will give teens some information on how to budget properly, understand needs versus wants, and decide which expenses are a priority.

4

HANDLING YOUR EXPENSES

As a teenager, learning the fundamentals of budgeting is important during your upbringing. The skill of budgeting enhances your financial stability. You will assume a better position to manage your money rather than letting it control you. With budgeting, you are less likely to incur impulse expenses, some of which are a result of peer pressure. There is much more that mastering the concept of budgeting can do for you. This chapter will cover various aspects of budgeting and the advantages that come with it.

BUDGETING: THE OVERVIEW

One thing you should know as a teenager is that a budget is a strategy for preplanning how you will spend your money each month. Designing such a strategy will help you see where your income comes from and how you spend it. This allows you to save more and stay clear of debt. By the way, it's not even complicated, as you will find out through this chapter! You simply need to know your expenses and income, to begin with.

Do Kids Really Need to Budget?

Learning how to budget at a young age could be a great attribute for you to acquire and practice. By the time you get older, you might have become a master of the skill. One of the financial skills that many people, even adults, find difficult to master is saving. However, it's not going to be so with you if you learn the art of budgeting now. This is because budgeting will allow you to allocate money for saving. Starting now, during your teenage years, will give you more time to practice these skills before adulthood knocks at your door.

Budgeting is a goal-oriented exercise because you plan how to use your money based on what you intend to achieve. Therefore, budgeting skills will automatically train you to set goals you'd want to achieve and design a plan on how to achieve them. These might be goals that are outside your financial bracket. If you want to be a "goal-getter," then learning how to budget also comes in handy.

Why Is Budgeting Important?

Do you want to understand the value of your money? Do you desire to live an organized financial life? Do you always wonder where your money is going as you send it randomly? Are you even wondering if your money can do something meaningful for you? Are you tired of those "Oh, why did I buy this" moments? The solution to all these issues and more is budgeting. Once you are able to budget well, then you become your money's boss. It sounds great, doesn't it?

Budgeting will help you avoid misusing your money. It also makes it easier for you to plan for the future. Budgeting makes it possible for you to create an emergency fund, where you can save up to three months of expenses in advance. The amount to save is more likely to depend on the cost of your current expenses.

WANTS VERSUS NEEDS

Needs are things that you cannot live without in your day-to-day living. These include water, a place to live, clothes, and food. Things that you can live without, though you sometimes claim that you need them, are known as wants. For example, the latest iPhone, name-brand sneakers, and an extra-large burger are all wants. Understanding the difference between a want and a need can be tricky in everyday life, as it is easy to categorize your wants as needs.

The "marshmallow test" was taken to study how long a child can wait to be given something. Stanford University was the first to set up this study in the 1970s (Lee, 2021). The study distinguished if children can tell the difference between a need and a want. A child would be given one marshmallow if they couldn't wait longer but two of them if they could.

Based on this study, if kids could wait for a long-term reward, which might not necessarily be a marshmallow, then they can forego the immediate gratification that comes with wants and be determined to get their needs covered instead. Being able to differentiate between your needs and wants helps you to manage cravings that might affect long-term goals. This means that you will be able to save for something that you want or need without falling into the trap of using the money on something else.

Once you can separate the two meanings between a need and a want, you'll eventually be able to manage where your money is going. As you grow into adulthood, you'll find it easy to prioritize the important things first, such as paying rent, as compared to going out with friends. Please note that all this does not mean that wants are not important. Going out with your friends is a crucial part of your social, mental, and emotional life. However, you need to put your priorities in place, and in most cases, your needs will need your first attention.

Here are some of the common needs that relate to you as a teenager:

- Water
- Security
- Food
- Utilities
- Clothes
- Shelter
- Medication
- Transportation
- Helping parents with rent

The following might be your wants:

- Entertainment
- Socializing
- Games
- Shopping
- Latest electronic gadgets
- Eating out
- Travel
- Designer clothes

THE BUDGET PRACTICE

Budgeting is a practical skill that you should practice in your everyday life. There are certain things that you should include if you are to create a good budget. This section expounds on these vital budget components.

Income

In order to create a budget plan, the first thing is to know how much money you receive. Is there something that brings in money for you? For instance, a part-time job or house chores. Make a list of where your income comes from, then from there, write down the total amount you receive in a month. If your income is irregular each month, then it is best for you to estimate your total pay at an average amount to avoid overvaluing.

Expenses

There are two categories under which expenses are listed. These are "fixed expenses," which should remain the same every month, and "variable expenses," which tend to change.

Examples of fixed expenses are your rent, phone bill, vehicle insurance, gym membership, and iTunes subscription. Expenses such as outings, food, vacations, and transport fall under your variable costs. Variable expenses are normally expenses you have control over. For example, you can choose to cook at home, which is often cheaper than buying food in restaurants. This way, you alter a variable expense. However, you cannot decide to change the amount of rent that you pay where you are living, so you cannot alter fixed expenses.

Spending

What do you spend your money on? You need to follow up on your expenses so that you have a better understanding of what you use your money for. Here are some of the probable expenses that you might realize upon tracking your spending habits:

- Gas costs
- Telephone bill
- Car repairs
- Extra expenses (like toiletries)
- Netflix subscription
- Gym membership
- Junk food
- Latest shoes and jewelry
- Hair and nail services
- Outings and hobbies

If you still live with your parents, you might not need to include rent on your list. However, if you help out with bills at home, do add them as important spending expenses. Add more items to this list so that it reflects your personal expense sheet.

Among all the costs that you may list, you will realize that the importance of expenses is not the same. Therefore, you can classify them into "necessary" and "other" expenses. Your electricity bills and rentals are necessary expenses, while gym membership, outings, and the latest fashion clothes fall under "other" expenses.

Goals

Your budget and goals correlate with each other. If you have a goal that you want to achieve, then you need to budget for it. Similarly, if you budget for something, that thing becomes a goal. Your budget can be one of the best sources of motivation for achieving your goals. Let's say you are planning on going on a vacation during the holidays. Having that plan set up will motivate you to stick to your budget so that when the time comes, you'll have enough money to go for that vacation. No matter how large your goals may be, you are bound to achieve them as long as you stick to your budget. It might take longer, depending on the costs involved and your income, but the bottom line is that you will love to celebrate achieving your goals.

Habits

Writing down all of your spending habits is another way to help you create a sound budget. You can download a printable habit tracker to help you follow up on all of your spending patterns by the end of the week. Tracking your habits will help you to see if there is any unnecessary spending that you may cut off so that you can save more. For instance, if you realize that you are always buying takeout for lunch, maybe to save more, you might want to try making your own lunch at home. That small improvement to your habits may save you more money. If there is something that you use more often, you could try buying in bulk than in singles. The money that you save each time might seem small, but check it out after a long stretch of time, and you will be shocked at how much you would have saved through a minor change in your habits.

STRATEGIES FOR BUDGETING

Now that you know what you intend to do with your money, it's time to allocate certain amounts of money to each item. There are many strategies that you may employ to get this done. We will enlighten you on some of these in this section.

The 50/30/20 Rule

There are multiple budgeting methods, but one of the most used methods is the 50/30/20 rule. When using this plan, 20% of your budget goes to your savings, 30% covers your wants, and the rest is meant for your needs. Although it's easier said than done, especially if your parents cover all of your needs, it is important to gain knowledge on saving during your early teenage years in order to prepare for the future. You can always make changes to how you manage your expenses as your salary increases.

Setting SMART Goals

Have you ever heard about SMART goals? Whether your answer is yes or no, setting your goals using the SMART approach gives you the edge to get them done. SMART is an acronym that represents specific, measurable, achievable, realistic, and time related. Therefore, as you create your goals, make sure they are

- **Specific:** In order to achieve your goal, it is best to work on one idea at a time. Know what you want to do. You could say, "I want to set up a business in the technology sector." This is more specific than saying, "I need to do something that gives me more money." Specificity is the key.
- **Measurable:** How are you going to measure your progress in the goals that you have set up? This has to be clear; otherwise, pursuing a goal when you can't evaluate your progress won't help much. If you want to start a business in the technology sector, have you taken steps to acquire the relevant knowledge? What have you done so far to show that you are getting there?

- **Achievable:** When working toward your goal, make sure you have a plan on how you are going to execute it. In fact, can that goal be achieved in the first place based on circumstances that are specific to you? Not everything that is achievable to someone else is equally possible for you. Set up goals that you can tackle. While setting up challenging goals may stretch your ability, ones that are too hard may also demotivate you in the long run when they don't materialize.
- **Realistic:** Is your whole plan realistic? You wouldn't want to create a fictional goal that you will never live to achieve. Stay within the boundaries of reality based on factors such as your attitude, environment, and available resources.
- **Time-related:** Set a time period for achieving your goal. This will motivate you to work hard enough. In the technology business example, you could decide to do it by the time you reach nineteen. You could even say, "In the next three years, I should have set up my business in the technology sector."

Zero-Based Budgeting

Zero-based budgeting mainly emphasizes that every amount in your account should be categorized. Using the zero-based budgeting system allows you to track what you spend your money on. The difference between the normal way to budget and the zero-based budgeting is that the regular budget permits you to leave your extra money in your checking account. However, when you use the zero-based budget plan, you will need to move your extra money into other plans. As a result, the balance after budgeting, in this case, is always zero. An investment calculator can help you determine how to divide your paycheck into your different plans.

In addition to classifying your expenditures, you need to identify your financial goals for either settling all of your debts or saving for something else. Whether it's saving for a new car or putting money aside for traveling, all these expenses should be listed in your expenditure. The balance in your checking account will help you determine how much you will need to set aside for every expense. You can also obtain an approximate amount through your credit card and bank statement.

The zero-based budget is great for people with an unstable income, which may be the case with you. The advantage of a zero-based budget is that you can tell your expenses by looking at your previous salary. When you do so, this allows you to use what you have left at your disposal. After laying out your budget, you need to deduct the expenses from your monthly income. In instances where your expenses supersede your income, you will have to re-evaluate your budget and get rid of unnecessary expenses in order to have enough money for your savings. You can either opt for a higher-paying job or minimize your expenses by limiting unnecessary spending. It's also vital to develop yourself and further your skills to advance in your career, which will allow you to earn a higher income. This will give you room to save more and cater to most of your expenses.

However, it is important to note that every surplus needs to be allocated to your expenditures. If you don't allocate the extra money you have left, there is a possibility of you spending it on unnecessary things when you could have used it for something more valuable. That is the principle behind zero-based budgeting. Considering that expenses may not be as consistent, you will need to re-evaluate your zero-based budget when necessary. Do not get yourself worked up by that; the re-evaluation process is simple. All you should do is make a few changes to your expenditures whenever there are new developments.

The 70/20/10 Budgeting Strategy

Budgeting for all of your necessities and outings can be challenging. The 70/20/10 rule is one of the methods people prefer to use since it is less complicated. Here's how to implement it:

The 70/20/10 splits your income into percentages to cover all three of your categories. The largest amount, which is 70%, covers things that you cannot live without, such as a roof under your head. Then, 20% covers any debts you may have outstanding. If all of your debts are paid, then this money goes to your savings. After all of the important things are covered, the remaining 10% is there to cater for all your trips, outings, or extra things you might want to get yourself.

THE MILLIONAIRE HABITS

Truth be told, the majority of us don't get paid a million within a year. We might not even inherit a large sum of assets. However, it doesn't mean that it is impossible to achieve a million. Being young is an advantage because then you'll still have more time to retire a millionaire. You need to budget and spend like a millionaire if you want to do that. In essence, you should strive to develop the relevant millionaire habits that we will describe in this section.

Stop Unnecessary Shopping

One habit people have is buying things they don't need, and teenagers are not an exception. It is easy to assume that only expensive items are the cause of poor budgeting. However, every expense, even as little as buying coffee, contributes to not being able to save money. You need to be disciplined in your spending. This will mean sacrificing most of the things you like so you can save more.

Avoid Expensive Cars

There's no problem with buying an expensive car. However, keep in mind that deciding to buy an expensive car that is way past your budget is like falling into your own trap because cars usually lose value in a matter of time. A new car may lose up to 15% to 20% of its value per year, depending on what kind of car it is and the demand rate. In conclusion, if you're still young, it is best to buy a car you can pay for in cash, or that has a low monthly installment. This way, in the years to come, you would have saved more and invested in assets with more value.

THE BOTTOM LINE

There's no need to depend on a lottery to have a large sum of money in your name. For some individuals, long-term saving is the only way to retire a millionaire. Just remember that there's no need to live a poor life to achieve your millionaire retirement plan. If you start at a young age and budget well, you will become a millionaire in time. The table below can serve as a template for creating your budget. Fill in as many items as you can, as long as they are applicable to your life.

Teen budget table for monthly expenses:

Budget component	Saved amount ($)	Used amount ($)
Fixed costs		
1. College fees		
Total	$	$
Variable costs		
1. Food		
Total	$	$
Grand total	$	$

From the total income that you have, subtract the budgeted costs so that you get the amount of money that you intend to save. At the end of the month, subtract the total money that you actually spent so that you get the see the real savings or debt that you have. This will help you to adjust your budget for the next month accordingly.

Well done for taking the time to learn important aspects of handling your money in this chapter. The journey continues in the next chapter as you get a better insight into credit cards, what you can do with them, and which is the best one to apply for.

5

THE SECRETS OF THE CREDIT CARD

Upon opening a bank account, being able to apply for and have access to a credit card is one of the benefits you will be able to enjoy. This chapter will take you through everything you need to know about credit cards, how they have made an impact on the world, and the types of credit cards that are available. You will also be educated on how you can apply for a credit card. A credit card is a device that you can get from the bank if you have a bank account, and it allows you to buy goods and services by just swiping it. You can also pay your bills and school fees using a credit card as long as the institute has a swiping machine. Credit cards have made an impact on the way people view spending and saving. They allow you to buy things and then pay back the money later. When it comes to the advantages of having a credit card, convenience takes first place. Credit cards have had positive effects on the economy. The demand for hard cash has decreased over the years due to the increased usage of credit cards, and this reduces friction in the economy.

CREDIT CARDS: THE OVERVIEW

Credit cards have made things like shopping, paying bills, or getting cash back relatively easier. There is no question that having a credit card is now necessary in this modern world. Let's dive deep into more detail about credit cards.

What Is a Credit Card?

A credit card is a device that you are given by a bank in order for you to pay for your goods and services and then pay the bank later. This device can be metal, but in most cases, it is plastic, and you can use it simply by swiping.

Do Teens Really Need Credit Cards?

Nothing is as tempting as being able to buy anything you want on credit. Credit cards are often blamed for bankruptcy due to the access to credit that you can easily abuse if you don't practice discipline. The truth is, if handled properly, credit cards come with more positives than negatives. Having said this, as a teen, you do need credit cards. They teach you how to handle credit, which is a skill that will come in handy when you finally become an independent adult. You will learn about bill payments and why it is important to pay them on time to avoid being penalized. Credit cards will also assist in cases of emergencies like medical or car issues when you are not in possession of money. They will bring you convenience and many other amazing benefits that you cannot afford to miss.

What Is the Difference Between a Credit Card and a Debit Card?

A lot of people are often confused about credit cards and debit cards. They find it difficult to decide which one will best suit their needs. If you are one of those people, this section will be of much help to you because it will highlight the main difference between the two.

When you use a credit card, you are using money that is borrowed from the bank, while when you use a debit card, money will be deducted directly from your bank account. On a credit card, money will be taken from your account at a later stage, but with a debit card, money is instantly withdrawn from your account. A credit card comes with rewards, points, and discounts, but a debit card does not offer these leverages. Debit cards will not help you build your credit history, but credit cards do. Also, note that credit cards come with higher interest rates and fees as compared to debit cards. Understanding this will help you to apply relevant caution when you are dealing with credit cards. Therefore, maximize the benefits and do the best that you can to cut down on the negatives of owning a credit card.

WHAT TEENS CAN DO WITH A CREDIT CARD

Using borrowed money from a bank through a credit card might seem to be a big deal, but wait until you learn other things that you can do with your card. Credit cards come with many benefits that you will enjoy. Let's explore some of these benefits in this section.

Start Building a Credit Score

Other than credit cards, nothing else will help you build your credit score. All credit card issuers are constantly sending account holders' credit histories to the national credit bureaus. These credit bureaus are Equifax, Experian, and TransUnion. All those credit reports will go straight to your record, and that's how your credit score is built.

Use in Emergencies

Imagine getting stuck in the middle of nowhere with a flat tire or because you are out of gas and are far from home. What a relief it will be when you notice your credit card sticking out of your wallet. You can use it, in this case, to get out of this situation. Falling ill is one of those unexpected emergencies that you might come across, and your credit card will assist you in paying four medical bills if you do not have money. You can also use your credit card to make that critical funeral policy payment.

Earn Rewards for Your Spending

With a credit card, you can earn rewards in the form of airline miles, points, cash back, and many other forms. There are ways through which you can increase your chances of getting rewards with your credit card. In most cases, credit cards will make you earn rewards when you spend a certain amount of money on specific goods and services. You need to be constantly checking your credit card issuer's website so that you are always aware if there are any promotions on certain goods so that you can maximize your spending on them to earn rewards. There are also what are called "sign-up bonuses." These are offered to you when you spend a certain amount over a certain period of time just after becoming an active member of your credit card issuer.

Utilize Cash-Back Offers

Cash back is money that you are given back by your credit card issuer after spending a certain amount of money. Cash back works like discounts in that it is a percentage of your spending that you are given back. You need to make sure that you pay the remaining amount in full by the end of the month; otherwise, the interest you will be charged will overwhelm the cash back you are supposed to be getting. Usually, you will get your cash back at the end of the month or at the end of the year. It all depends on your credit card. However, be wary of credit card companies that promise cash-back rewards to entice you to spend more than you can afford.

THE INS AND OUTS OF A CREDIT SCORE

For a lot of people, the term "credit score" rings a bell, but they have no idea what it means. You should know, though, that a credit score is a powerful aspect that can greatly impact your financial history. Let us have a look at what a credit score is and how it affects your credit history.

What Is a Credit Score?

A credit score is like a summary of your credit history, spending habits, and how quickly or late you pay back the money that you would have spent. There is a scoring formula that companies use in order to determine your credit score. The scores are three-digit numbers, with 300 being the lowest, 800 being the highest in VintageScore, and 850 being the highest in FICO. Your credit score is found by dividing the number of days in a specific period, say, 30 days in a month, by the receivables turnover for that specific period. Receivables turnover is the number of times your credit card issuer will collect the money you would have spent with your credit card from you every year.

Why Teens Need to Understand Credit Scores From an Early Age

Credit scores are permanently recorded in your financial credit history for life. This is a serious issue that you should never take lightly. As a teen, you need to understand that your credit score will greatly affect you in the long run. So, by understanding that from an early age, you can make wise decisions and make sure that you grow up with a good credit score.

What is the Role of a Credit Score for a Teen?

A credit score will determine how trustworthy you are. It shows credit card issuers if you are able to pay the money back on time. If your credit score shows that you pay money back on time, you gain the leverage to apply for any type of credit card that you want. As you become an adult, you will put yourself in a position of choosing any credit card you want because you will need them the most then.

What are the Future Consequences of a Bad Credit Score?

As mentioned above, with a good credit score, you will have unlimited choices when it comes to applying for credit cards. However, with a bad credit score, you do not get the chance to choose. You will just end up picking any credit card issuer that will approve your application if any. A bad credit score will make credit card issuers hesitant to do business with you because they will worry that you will inconvenience them by not paying their money back on time.

GETTING A CREDIT CARD

Getting a credit card can prove to be a bit of a difficult process for teens because they usually have limited sources of money, and they might not be of legal age. Here, we will mention four of the best credit cards that you are eligible for as a teenager.

Student Cash Back from Discover It

Discover It Student Cash Back does not have a specific spending reward. However, you can claim your rewards at the end of the year. You can redeem your rewards any way you want to. You can choose to shop on Amazon and get huge discounts as well. You are guaranteed to get a response within 30 to 60 minutes of applying for this credit card online. There is no need for proof of income if you are a teenager or a student.

Bank of America Travel Rewards Credit Card for Students

This credit card comes with a sign-up bonus, so you will earn points if you spend a certain amount of money in the first 90 days after becoming an active member. The Bank of

America Travel Rewards credit card for students comes with a 16.24% APR but no annual fee (Resendiz, 2017). This credit card is best if you travel a lot because it comes with zero foreign transaction fees. It also offers rewards in the form of car rental services, plane tickets, hotel stays, and many others.

Deserve EDU Mastercard for Students

Deserve EDU Mastercard for Students has a sign-up bonus when you spend up to $500 within your first three months. This credit card also comes with an APR of 20.99% (Resendiz, 2017). Deserve EDU Mastercard for Students comes with no foreign transaction fees and no annual fees. This credit card is best for teenagers who want to start their financial journey, as it does not require a credit score for you to apply.

Blue Cash Everyday Card From American Express

The Blue Cash Everyday Card from American Express is one of the best-rewarding credit cards available. You can earn up to two percent in cash back when you spend money on things like gas and dining. When you are a new member, you will get double these rewards, depending on your security deposit. This credit card does not come with an annual fee. This means your account will not be affected if you do not use it often.

LESSONS TO LEARN WITH CREDIT CARDS

Before applying for a credit card, there are various important lessons you need to learn so that you do not find yourself on the unfortunate side. These lessons will help you know if you are ready to take on the responsibility of a credit card. These lessons are listed and explained in this section.

Lesson 1: You Need to Understand How Credit Cards Work

Most teens find themselves in serious debt because they get the impression that credit card money is free money. The right thing to do is to treat credit card money like a loan that needs to be paid back. Make sure that you do not overspend that money because exceeding your limit might come with a penalty. You also need to understand that interest is money you are required to pay for the loaned money. And the more credit card money you spend, the more interest you will be required to pay. Literally, you will be offering the bank free money, not vice versa.

Before applying for a credit card, be sure to know the terms and conditions that it comes with. You need to be familiar with terms like annual fee, annual percentage rate (APR), balance transfers, cash advance, rewards rate, foreign transaction fees, and welcome bonus. An annual fee is an amount that you will be charged for using a credit card, and you pay this amount at the end of each year. This fee is usually charged for credit cards that come with special benefits like rewards. An APR is the interest you will pay if you are late on your bill payment. APR comes in three main types, which are penalty APR, balance transfer intro APR, and purchase intro APR. These three types of APR are quite self-explanatory. Penalty APR is associated with late payments of bills. Balance transfer intro APR will be charged when you transfer your money from one account to another. Then, purchase intro APR will depend on your spending.

Balance transfers are transactions you make when you want to transfer debt from a certain account to another account. People usually transfer debt to an account with low or no interest rates. A cash advance is almost the same as taking cash from an ATM, but it comes with an APR and transaction fees. A reward rate is like a token of appreciation that a credit card will offer you in the form of miles, cash back, or points. A foreign transaction fee is a fee that you will be charged for making transactions when you are outside the United States. It is best to look for a credit card that charges low foreign transaction fees if you travel a lot.

A welcome bonus is offered to new members of a credit card. You can only earn this bonus when you make transactions that amount to a specific amount of money. This bonus will come in the form of miles, points, or cash back.

Lesson 2: Be Aware of How Your Credit Card Use is Linked to Your Credit Score

How you use your credit card will definitely make an impact on your credit score. Your credit score lets companies know how well you handle loans. With a bad credit score, credit card issuers will charge you high interest rates or not enroll you at all.

Lesson 3: Start Slow With Your Credit Card

The best thing to do when you have just opened a credit card is to start slow. Spend within your means so that when the time for paying it back comes, you will not have any issues. Getting carried away and going all out will lead you into huge debt that might be difficult to pay back. Late payments will come with penalties and will also affect your credit score.

Lesson 4: You Need to Understand What Interest Means With Credit Cards

Interest is like the money that you are charged for borrowing credit card money. You need to be very careful with the amount of money you spend with your credit card. You will be charged interest according to the amount that you spend. The larger the amount, the higher the interest.

CHOOSING A CREDIT CARD

When it comes to choosing which credit card to open, there are things that you should take into consideration. You need to choose a credit card that will be able to meet all your needs. To further explain this, we will give references to some questions you should ask yourself before choosing a credit card.

- Are you just starting your credit journey?
- Will you be able to pay the APR and interest?
- Will you be able to pay back the money?
- Do you want to earn points?
- Do you have a good credit score?
- Do you want to pay your debt with a credit card?

MILLIONAIRE HABITS

Have you ever wondered why there is such a huge gap between the rich and the poor in some states? A lot of people wonder why millionaires stay rich while some people remain poor. It all comes down to spending habits, especially with their credit cards. Let us look at some habits that are practiced by millionaires that you should consider adding into your daily financial routine. These habits won't make you a millionaire overnight, but they surely will improve your financial situation over time. Millionaires

- use their cards whenever they can
- pay back loans in due time
- take advantage of reward credit cards
- make use of bonuses that come with spending habits that are high
- usually, go for quality credit cards that come with no annual fee

As you are progressing through the chapters, you are being educated on how you can be a responsible adult financially. This chapter took you through credit cards, why they are important, how they contribute to your financial history, and how they can teach you responsibility. After opening a credit card and building up a good credit score, you will find yourself with some extra money in your account. You need to make wise decisions with this money and use it accordingly. The next chapter will teach how you can be responsible with money by educating you on the importance of investing and how you can go about it.

6

SHAPE YOUR FUTURE AND INVEST

Investment has no age limit. As a matter of fact, it is even better for you to start investing at a younger age. Investment is a productive way to make your money work for you and conceivably build massive wealth. While most people start investing as adults, investing as a teen will give you an edge, just like Brandon Fleisher had.

At 13, Brandon Fleisher developed an affinity for stocks after his math teacher asked students to pick a stock and monitor it to see how it performed. He began trading fake stocks and became successful at it. Brandon's parents were supportive enough to give him $48,000 from their savings so that he could invest. Unlike most people, Brandon did not choose the large-cap stocks but rather went for Avalon Rare Metals (AVL). The stock tripled his investments from $48,000 to $147,000 in just two years! Who knows? Maybe, you could be the next Brandon of your time if you gather the bravery to start investing. This chapter will give you valuable information on various aspects of investing and the opportunities that come with it.

THE INVESTING OVERVIEW

Investing may sound complex, but in simple terms, it is the process of buying assets that gradually increase in value over some time. It can also be defined as the selling of assets that decrease in value over time, thereby generating an increase in your original capital. Investing is a great tool that helps you to grow your money and be in a better position to meet your desired financial goals. When you invest your money, it is more likely to give you returns. All investments carry some degree of risk, but depending on where you put your money, your returns are either guaranteed or market-linked.

With guaranteed returns, there is a fixed amount that you receive at the beginning of the investment. Market-linked returns provide you with the option to invest in equities and debt markets. Every investor wishes to have great returns, so many would opt for equity markets since they are the most likely to provide high returns, but the downside to these markets is they carry higher risk. If you are looking for stable returns and low-risk scenarios, we recommend that you go for debt markets. A simple investing principle that you may need to consider is the longer you hold to your investments, the greater the chances of reaping higher returns. Keep this tip; it may come in handy someday.

Teens and Investing

Financial services are mainly offered to adults because they have the mental ability to comprehend and handle these issues. Teens, however, are allowed to invest under the guidance and surveillance of their parents. Teens are prohibited from opening their brokerage accounts as long as they are below 18. To invest as a teen, your parents should open a brokerage account for you.

Benefits of Investing as a Teen

Teenagers who start investing early have a big edge over their peers. You have the potential to accumulate more returns and acquire knowledge from investing so that by the time you reach adulthood, you will have achieved most of your financial goals.

Age is your biggest and most valuable asset. This is because it gives you the lead compared to adults who start investing at a later stage. The underlying principle here is that the earlier you invest, the longer and quicker you put the compound effect into play. The compound effect is the ability of your money to start working on its own. This means that your interest in your original investments will begin to also accumulate more interest.

The broader perspective here is that in the future, your investments will help you pay for your future expenses like traveling the world, college funds, capital for your business, and much more. Interestingly, one study showed that 53% of Americans consider their finances to be a source of anxiety, with respondents whose ages ranged from 18 to 34 reporting the highest levels of stress (FINRA, 2018). Taking this initiative early will help you feel more confident and reduce anxiety about money issues afterward. You would rather be part of the minority who worries less about money issues.

THE BASICS OF INVESTING

Once investing is mentioned, many people think of the stock market. Stock investing is just one form of investing, but the whole aspect of investing is much broader. In fact, investing is simply devoting money to a specific undertaking with the expectation of getting a reward in the future. Investments can earn money in different ways, like appreciation, compounding, and dividends. Risk tolerance is another important aspect as far as investing is concerned. We will discuss all these components of investing in this section.

Appreciation

This is when you buy an asset, and it increases in value over time. By the time you sell the asset, it will be worth more than when you bought it. This way, you earn from your investments. Please note that it is also possible for assets that you invest in to lose value as time progresses. This usually happens in periods of recession in the economy. However, down-movements of asset values do not last forever, so they will still appreciate in value.

Compound Interest

Compounding is one of the fastest ways to make your money grow faster. As a teen, time is on your side, so you should make the most out of this concept. With compound interest, your money grows faster than your initial investment. You might be confused by how this principle works, but we will explain it here. When you earn interest on your initial investment, it's up to you to take them out of your earnings or rather reinvest them. If you choose the latter, your preceding interest will be calculated on your initial investment, as well as on the additional interest investment. In essence, you will be making money on what you put in, plus what you pick up along the way.

To make you understand the concept of compound interest in a more theoretical way, let's take a look at this scenario. Let's suppose that you invest $2,000 and it has 10% interest every year; this means you will have made $2,200 in the first year. At the end of two years, you will have $2,420. To break it down, this means that during your second year, you not only earn $200 from your $2,000 investment, but you also earned $10 from the $100 interest that you accumulated in the first year. This is the miracle behind compound interest.

More compound interest is earned over long stretches of time. This is where your young age becomes an advantage. You can make long-term investments and allow them to accumulate compound interest. The shorter the investment, the lower the chances of earning much from compounding.

Dividends

These are specifically for stock investments. You invest in a certain stock of a company, and they pay you a percentage of their earnings based on the number of shares you own in that company. Basically, when you invest in the stocks of a company, you are buying shares from it. This means that you become a shareholder. This means that you are also an owner of the company's assets and earnings. When the issuing company makes profits, these are divided among all the shareholders. These profits are distributed as dividends. Therefore, dividends are a relatively passive way of earning from your investments, considering that you don't have to buy and sell assets to earn them. Please note that there are some companies that do not offer dividends.

Risk Tolerance

Risk tolerance defines your capacity and preparedness to remain calm when your investments go through the dips of market trends. The best way to determine your risk is by asking yourself if you are willing to maintain your positions when the market dips. There is no harm in knowing and confirming that you have low risk tolerance. It actually helps you to know the types of investments that you can undertake. This is because risk levels vary with different investments. Many investors have different psychological strengths and weaknesses, so it is very important to understand and study how you handle market crashes mentally.

The Importance of Risk Tolerance

Risk tolerance exempts you from worrying a lot about your money every day. If you don't have the guts to deal with the risk of losing your investment, then the best choice would be to settle for lower-risk investments and the unfavorable lower returns that accompany them. For investments that have the potential to yield higher returns, the risk involved is relatively high. The possibility that you may experience an outright loss when you are dealing with such investments is quite high.

The bigger picture is to earn higher returns from your investments, but worrying about the volatility will hinder you from making the right decisions. You need to develop risk tolerance that will put you in a mental state that allows you to remain calm, no matter the fluctuations in the market. The less you worry about your investments, the more you make the best decisions.

Diversity

Diversification is about reducing risk and increasing the chance of making higher returns by investing in different assets in one portfolio. This brings balance to your investments in case you lose money from one asset type. Diversification shields you from losing all your investments at once since the positive returns of some investments neutralize the negative returns of some investments.

The reason why this technique is effective is that a portfolio made up of different asset types will yield higher returns in the future. On the other hand, diversification reduces the risk of any individual holding. This is when risk tolerance comes into play; you also have to include how much time you have before you cash out your investments. Being a teen gives you the time and space to make higher-risk investments because you will have a long way to go before retirement. The ample time that you have allows you to handle a certain amount of unpredictability in the short term, possibly earning more returns on your investment in the long term.

TYPES OF INVESTMENTS

Focusing on one type of investment can build your wealth. Engaging in various types of investments will put the odds in your favor and increase your chance of building massive wealth as well. If you don't learn the different types of investments that apply to you, you will find it difficult to determine what to go for. This section focuses on expounding on various types of investments, including the features and risks that are associated with them.

Roth IRA

As a teenager, you can open a Roth IRA, but you should have a job that gives you a low tax rate. A Roth IRA is by far one of the best investments for teens, and it teaches you the skill of how to save for the future. A Roth IRA, in layman's terms, is an individual account that you invest in to save money for retirement. The advantage of investing in a Roth IRA is that your money will grow and be withdrawn without any tax charges. The minimum number of years before you are allowed to withdraw from your Roth IRA account is five years. Money that goes into your Roth IRA has a tax fee, but the withdrawals are tax-free.

Index Funds

Index funds are a kind of mutual fund that seeks to track the returns of a market index like the S&P 500. Index funds come with a big market exposure, reduced expenses, and a low portfolio gross revenue. Regardless of the market, state index funds will always follow their benchmark index. Previously, we talked about Roth IRA accounts as beneficial for teenagers, but index funds are superior savings for your retirement. Warren Buffet, the most famous investor, prefers to use index funds because they are the safest saving method. The power of this kind of investment is they save you from the highs and lows of investing in one company.

Stocks

Stocks are also known as equity, which is the value of shares issued by a company. Owning a share means you have ownership of a fraction of the company you bought the stock from. Shares are the units of stocks that give you the right to own a proportion of the corporation's assets and profit equal to how much stock you own. Investing in stocks will heighten your awareness of what's happening around the economy. Most companies have high-priced stocks, so you should save before you invest in the stock market.

The stock exchange market is where you buy and sell stocks. This is the foundation of most individual investors' portfolios. As a stock trader, you should obey government rules and regulations that guard you against illegal practices.

Investing in a Business

A more exciting investment is putting your money into a business. Some businesses are designed to take advantage of people, so you should diligently do your research before investing in any business. You can also consult your parents to give you expert guidance on the businesses that you can invest in. Investing in a business will trigger your willingness to learn more about investing and business quickly, as you are more actively involved in most of the decision-making. The cost of investing in a business can be too high, so you want to ensure that you are very well-educated about the business you are investing in before you part with your money.

Certificates of Deposit

Certificates of deposit (CDs) are savings account types where you can keep a specific amount of money for a stipulated period of time, even up to five years. The bank that issues CDs gives interest on the held money. CDs are not as appealing to teenagers compared to stocks, but they are also a very good investment option to consider. The day you decide to cash in your CD, you receive the original amount that you invested plus the interest that accumulated over that period.

CDs are more like bonds and are the safest savings options. You should read and understand thoroughly the disclosure statement of the specific CD that you are dealing with. The disclosure statement informs you of the interest rate the bank is willing to pay. It also gives information on whether the interest is fixed or variable. In this statement, the bank will mention the period it will pay the interest on the CD, for example, monthly, annually, or after five years. CDs have a maturity date, which represents the minimum amount of time after which you are allowed to withdraw your money. The bank should clearly state the penalties that come with violating this rule. The risk with CDs is that inflation will grow faster than your money, and your returns will be lower over time.

CDs are an excellent lesson on how investing money for a long period is beneficial, but early withdrawals can penalize you. The concept of compound interest also applies perfectly well to CDs.

INVESTING SKILLS FOR TEENAGERS

Every investor wants to build wealth, but the number one hindrance is the interference of emotions during market dips. In investing, there are two powerful emotions, which are greed and fear. Most of your success in investing relies on your ability to control these two emotions. You should study your habits and see which approach to investing goes with your personality. In addition, this helps you to choose whether you should go for an aggressive or conservative approach to investing. An aggressive approach can give high returns quickly but carries a lot of risks. A conservative approach is safe on paper, but sometimes you end up missing a lot of good opportunities and returns in the future. To sharpen your investing skills, here are a few questions to ask yourself.

How Do I Rate My Level of Knowledge and Experience in Investing?

If your knowledge is limited, then you should seek more before you invest in any asset. Investing without the right knowledge and experience may cost your savings. You can improve your skills by reading more books and practicing using demo accounts. When you are ready and more experienced, you can then make a decision on which investment type you want. If you are an expert, then you can venture more into other investments, not just large-cap stocks.

What's My Main Plan for Investment Growth?

If you are not sure of which investment plan to take, then you should do more research and homework before taking any action. If you decide to take a conservative and safer method, always consider that to make more money, you should beat inflation and take risks to grow your money in the future. As a teen, both a moderate and conservative approach can be good, considering you have time to grow your money so that by the time you reach adulthood, you will be in a good financial position. Teenagers love instant gratification, so an aggressive approach could be enticing. This approach can be tempting with its high rewards, but always calculate your risk against your risk tolerance levels.

What is the Nature of Your Current and Future Income Sources?

Investing is a game of probabilities. If your income and finances are unstable, investing in a balanced portfolio is the best choice. Alternatively, you can save and invest when you are in a more stable financial position. Most teens are not financially stable, so balanced portfolios would be the way to go for them.

Are You on Course With Your Goals Based on Your Age and Income?

Since you are a teenager, you have no pressure to take aggressive methods. If you plan to be wealthy by the time you reach adulthood, taking conservative methods is a good choice. You can save money for some time and then invest in any method that you desire. Confidence can blind you to making irrational decisions if you are in a good financial position, so always keep a balanced portfolio and grow your money.

How Much of Your Holdings Are in Stocks?

Depending on your risk tolerance, it is good to have a portfolio that is all stocks since you have a long time before you need the money. Half stocks and other investments are good alternatives because they bring balance to your investments.

What Kinds of Stocks Do You Own?

Stocks are different, some are large-cap, and others are small-cap. Some have large growth potential, while others have small growth potential. Small-cap stocks carry a larger risk compared to large-cap stocks. You should always dig deep into the kind of stocks that you own. Doing this saves you from regretting it in the future. Large-cap stocks offer stability, but there is also no harm in going for small-cap stocks and mid-cap stocks to complement your existing holdings. Most people love to grow their money quickly, so they take high-growth stocks, but be aware that these carry the highest risk. If you do not have a backup stock plan, we recommend that you stay away from high-growth stocks. Diversification is always the perfect way to invest. You can invest in stocks, bonds, and CDs to spice up your portfolio with diversity.

THE GOLDEN RULES OF INVESTING

Just like every game, investing has its own rules. These rules guide and help you to make the best decisions every step of the way. This section introduces five simple guidelines that will assist you in making better decisions.

- **Think of the long-term perspective.** Having a long-term perspective helps you to choose a liquidity preference. The recommended investment duration is about six months. You can demand a higher premium on long-term investments as opposed to short-term ones.

- **Never get derailed from focusing on the future.** Investing is a game of odds. You might think of finding ways to outsmart the market but forget about trying to pick winners all the time. All investment types have bad and good periods. Never expect the same return from the same investment. This kind of behavior will affect your decision-making. Keep an eye on the future.
- **Diversification.** Diversifying your portfolio will neutralize your investments. Having different asset classes will increase the chances of higher returns on your investment instruments. One investment asset cannot meet all your needs. Moreover, a diversified portfolio spreads the investment risk across many assets, a scenario that gives you the edge to survive should things not go well with some investments.
- **Invest in things that trigger your interest.** When you invest in things that you like, you are more likely to do more relevant research that keeps you updated. You can easily follow up on trends, and the probability of making it is relatively high.
- **Stay clear on your goals.** When you invest, you should have some goals in place. What do you intend to do? Are you looking forward to retiring earlier? Do you want to raise money for your college years?

Whatever your reasons for investing are, remain focused on them. They will motivate you to do your best in the market.

BEST APPLICATIONS FOR INVESTING

The biggest tool you will use in investing is your investing application. Good applications must have low fees and effective tools to help you reach your financial goals effectively.

SoFi

Sofi was made to be an easy-to-use application, especially for beginners. The minimum amount to invest using SoFi is $1, and it has no commissions for trades. SoFi has automated investing, where it picks and manages all your ETFs for you for free.

> **+ Pros:** SoFi has no management fees, administrative fees, and no advisory. It offers unlimited access to a team of financial planners who can assist you. You can have up 10 portfolios diversified between low-cost ETFs.
> **− Cons:** The biggest downside to SoFi is that it does not offer tax loss harvesting, which is offered by many of its biggest competitors. This means if you invest with SoFi, it does not reduce the taxes owed on investment gains.

Ally Invest

This is a perfect application if you are too scared or not yet interested in investing. Ally Invest offers a custodial account that allows parental involvement. This app helps you build your portfolio, earn dividends, and work toward future financial goals like saving for college.

> **+ Pros:** Trading on Ally Invest means you will have low trading and non-trading fees. There is zero commission on most stocks and ETFs.
> **— Cons:** The margin rates could be lower.

Robinhood

Robinhood is a trailblazer in the non-commission brokerage model. This is a very solid choice for you as a beginner as you start to invest in your assets with zero commission. Robinhood offers more features in a premium account that costs $5 a month. If you want to use a free account, you can only trade stocks and ETFs.

> **+ Pros:** With Robinhood, you have access to Free US stock and ETF trading. The app also works with excellent mobile and web trading platforms. Opening the account is relatively fast and can be done digitally.
> **— Cons:** The disadvantage of Robinhood is it has limited educational material. As a teen and a beginner,

you need to consume as much knowledge as you can. Robinhood also has a limited product range. One major problem is they have weak customer service.

Stash

Stash is great for teenagers who are looking to improve their investing skills. It offers automatic investing options in case you do not want to trade manually. With Stash, you can invest in as many securities as you want for a minimum of $1. The starting fee for using Stash is $1.

> **+ Pros:** Stash contains a feature where it can automatically save and invest for you. Because of fractional shareholding, you can invest with a minimum of one cent. Portfolio suggestions are built to match the level of risk that you are exposed to. With Stash, all your trades will not accumulate any commission in the future.
> **− Cons:** The major downside with Stash is you have to pay a monthly fee. This has a more significant effect if you have a small account. Stash has no wealth management services, so if you decide to use it, you should manage your investments by yourself.

Acorns

Acorns is a great app for people who do not have the time to manage investments by themselves. As a teen, you might be occupied with a lot of schoolwork, so choosing Acorns may be a great decision. The app will manage your investments while you focus on other things. Acorns charges a fee of $3 a month to take care of everything. More services include automatic transactions, retirement account savings, and more.

> **+ Pros:** An excellent feature that Acorns has is its automatic savings account. This app also has great educational content. This is an advantage for you as a beginner, and also its additional perks.
> **− Cons:** Acorns charges fees based on the percentage of assets you have. Another disadvantage is that it has limited portfolio options, so you can only choose a few assets to put into your portfolio. It also incurs charges on every transaction of ETFs that you make, and this can be costly for you.

Ameritrade

Ameritrade is suitable for all kinds of traders, you included. Its wide range of educational tools is very helpful for you as a new investor. You have access to great customer service with the assistance that you dearly need. There is no need to deposit any balance to use Ameritrade. This is an advantage, in addition to its very low pricing, that allows you to be comfortable when investing in the market. Another bonus is Ameritrade has dynamic portfolio tools. Regardless of your experience levels, you can leverage a range of trading features that are customizable for your preferred strategies.

> **✛ Pros:** Ameritrade consists of a wide range of educational tools that make it easy for you to build confidence and expertise in the market. Trading tools and resources that enable you to go after any investment strategy consistently are also part of the package that you get through Ameritrade. The application is designed in a way that is easy to navigate, making it user-friendly for all kinds of investors.
> **━ Cons:** There are no fractional shares offered on Ameritrade. This hinders investors who are willing to add high-priced assets to their portfolios. Access to direct crypto trading is prohibited on this app. You can only trade cryptocurrencies using funds, Bitcoin futures, and over-the-counter trusts. You should manually enroll in the cash sweep program, thereby lifting your chances of missing out on interest.

Public

The stock market can appear intimidating for beginners to make life-changing decisions about investing on their own.

At first, even choosing stocks without proper guidance can be a little scary. This emphasizes the need for an effective application for you to learn more about the markets. Public offers social network features that make it possible for you to understand the markets better. You can also learn more from experienced investors on how they invest in their portfolios by following the Public feed. More interestingly, you can create a group to chat with other users and engage in live conversations.

+ **Pros:** Public allows you to buy and sell stocks and ETFs without having to pay a commission. You can purchase slices of an asset for as little as $1. The application offers lessons on investing, and then you earn free stock and crypto upon completion. You get to follow other investors using the Public feed, which makes it easier for you to learn from them. Communicating with them will enhance your skills as you can exchange strategies, discuss trends, and much more.

− **Cons:** Public only allows you to open cash accounts. No retirement or margin accounts are available. You are also limited to only investing in stocks, ETFs, and crypto.

CREATING A MOCK PORTFOLIO

The mock portfolio is a great way to practice and improve your investing skills. This is an account where you can buy and sell stocks, ETFs, and cryptocurrencies without using real money. This way, you can see how these assets perform over time without risking your money. A great way to get started is by coming up with a list of companies that you are excited about. We recommend you follow the stocks of big companies such as Disney, McDonald's, and Coca-Cola.

Make it a habit that every single day, week, or month you check the prices of these stocks and see how they are performing. Remember to record the latest prices. Keep yourself up to date by scanning newspapers, magazines, and other relevant websites so you can know the stories of the companies that you follow. Immediately after news reports, always check to see how the stocks in your mock portfolio react. Ask yourself if the stock went up or down so that you assess understanding.

Practice by applying simple math, such as pretending to buy 10 shares of a company's stock. How much did it cost you? To be more precise, always include broker commission in your calculations. Calculate your profit and return percentage after a few months.

As you venture and explore the stock market, you should consider how other school subjects, except math, are related to the stock market. There is history. It helps you to understand how big companies came from a small beginning to end up being the biggest companies in the world. In this modern era, there are progressively more technology companies that have big stocks. That is why it is important to study science subjects, which helps you to understand deeply about tech companies. Taking your English subject seriously will make it easy for you to read when you are researching stocks.

Since you are restricted from opening your brokerage account, you can do so with the help of your parents. You can open a joint brokerage account that you can use to buy shares together until you reach the age of 18.

MILLIONAIRE HABITS

To succeed, you need to have the right habits, specifically the ones that we call "millionaire habits." It is not easy to build or destroy bad habits because of the strong neural pathways in our brains. To be like a millionaire, you have to build powerful habits. Here are some of the most powerful habits millionaires follow.

- **Being conservative.** Millionaires have a healthy habit of saving more, spending less, and sticking to a budget. It is one of the greatest factors in why they can build wealth. In simple terms, millionaires live by a code of spending below their needs. They also invest their extra money so that it grows rather than spending it in a disorderly manner.

- **Saving.** Millionaires save most of their income. They understand that to build wealth, you have to save most of your income. Millionaires apply this concept, even in their investments. They put together strategies for shielding their investments and reducing the risk involved. That is why they employ strategies such as diversification.
- **Creating different streams of income.** It is possible to build your wealth with one source of income. However, most millionaires have different sources of income because it helps them build wealth exponentially. They can build wealth by creating sources of income in things they are talented in or passionate about. This explains why most of them also favor taking part in various forms of investing.
- **Real estate.** One of the most common investments made by millionaires is real estate. With real estate, you are exposed to benefits such as appreciation in houses over time. Moreover, you can get your returns without high tax charges.
- **Investing in low-index funds.** As we mentioned earlier, index funds have high returns but low risk. They are widely diversified because your portfolio is made up of different kinds of assets. Millionaires love index funds because of the low risk. You could also try this strategy.

- **They study and plan for future investments.** Most of the investments made by millionaires are fueled by their research. On average, millionaires spend more than 10.5 hours planning for investments every month. They understand that improving their financial literacy helps in making better investment decisions. You better do the same if you want to grow, especially financially.
- **Personal growth activities.** Millionaires spend more of their energy focusing on activities like reading and exercising. They are fully aware that to keep functioning at a high level, you have to invest in your emotional and cognitive resources. The emotional resilience that comes through exercising may come in handy during the dip moments of the market when investing.

With the vast knowledge that you have attained in this chapter, we recommend that you get ready to invest in preparation for your retirement, which will come in many years. To know how to do this, read the next chapter, which covers the nitty-gritty of retirement investments.

7

HERE COMES THE FUTURE

As is quite common, saving money is very important, because it cushions you in case of emergency. Saving for retirement comes in handy in the same way. Retirement is not an emergency, but should you live long, you will need to put aside enough to maintain your life. Retirement can be when one withdraws from their position of occupation or if they decide to reduce their working hours. Retirement may come because of age, that is, when someone has become elderly, or they cannot carry their workload because of health reasons.

It is very important for you to understand the importance of planning for your retirement. Lewis and Karen from Seattle planned for their retirement in a way that might be of interest. Karen worked for a consumer products company in New Jersey, while Lewis worked for the federal government.

Good planning and a well-structured pre-retirement lifestyle helped them to retire earlier since their after-retirement life was sufficiently insured. Currently, they are living their retirement dream in Seattle near their family.

According to them, they are now able to take good care of themselves after having given up their hectic careers. They have enough time to take daily walks, prepare healthy meals, and spend time with family and friends. They now do community volunteer work and have lots of time to bond with their two grandchildren. This is an indication of how good life can be if careful planning for retirement is done. This is all the more reason to start doing it at an early age.

THE RETIREMENT OVERVIEW

It is not quite common for teens to start thinking of retirement. In most cases, retirement saving begins with one's first full-time job, which may not be until one is in their twenties. It is, however, vital to have a head start on retirement savings and to do it as early as possible. Parents can help their teenagers to start planning for retirement because by starting early, they enjoy the benefits of saving for retirement. As a teenager, the earlier you begin, the better. While most babysitting and part-time gigs that you can do may not quite cut it in terms of saving up for retirement, you will most probably start proper part-time jobs while still in high school, and this is a good starting point (Sanders, 2018).

REASONS WHY TEENAGERS SHOULD START SAVING FOR RETIREMENT

It may not be easy to see the benefits of retirement savings unless they are explained clearly. There are a number of benefits to saving for retirement. These include:

- **Return on investment:** You can decide on the perfect investment tool that helps you to grow your money over time. Careful and proper planning of the required savings will help you to achieve your goals at a set time.
- **Financial backup in cases of emergencies:** After retirement, life becomes very unpredictable, and this can be frightening. Retirement saving makes sure that you are protected during financial emergencies.
- **Tax benefits**: When you invest in a plan that you select as suitable for you, you reduce your taxable income. This is a great relief on your source of income, while at the same time you are securing your future.
- **Peace of mind:** With retirement savings, you have peace of mind as you enter into a new phase of your life. You do not have to worry about what will happen to you if you are no longer working. It is very important to lay back and relax, knowing that your well-being is ensured.

- **Protection of assets and property:** People who do not save for retirement or start late usually find themselves in financial difficulties. They often have to resort to selling properties and assets to cover their financial needs. Saving early, therefore, cushions you from such financial disaster.
- **The early retirement option:** Saving for retirement gives you the option to retire early from your job. Many people find themselves having to work through old age or through ill health because if they do not work, they cannot sustain their livelihoods. In some cases, people become stuck if they are retrenched toward retirement.

From a young age, try as much as possible to develop the habit of saving. The advantages of saving for retirement at a young age include

- ensuring a good standard of living
- giving them flexibility
- creating a saving habit
- utilizing compound interest

PLANNING FOR RETIREMENT

Plans for retirement should be put in place carefully. Because of how fast paced the world has become, it is imperative that you should start planning your retirement early.

Understanding the power of time helps you to achieve success much easier. The teenage years are the perfect time for you to invest in yourself. This gives you a longer time frame to learn from your mistakes. Retirement planning that is done early is not only good for your finances, but it also helps your mental and physical health. Sometimes, it is best to invest and enjoy the fruits of your investments when you still have time and are still healthy to do so. Late in life may not be good enough. Let's look at some of the factors that affect retirement planning in this section.

Factor 1: Time Is of the Essence

One important factor when planning for retirement is age. You have to decide on an age threshold that helps you to make your decisions properly. You must remember that for anything you want to achieve in life, you have very limited time. Do not be caught in the same web that many people are caught in, that of believing that there is a best time to do something. They find themselves having waited their whole lives for that time. Starting your savings plan early gives you more time to compound your interest.

Factor 2: Find Your Spending Needs

Understanding your spending needs is very important for good retirement savings. This is because it helps you to determine how much income you are able to save at the end of every month. One good thing to incorporate into your savings is consistency when it comes to spending. This helps you to develop a solid plan and to stick to it.

Factor 3: Grow Your Financial Education

Retirement planning is all about careful calculations of your time as well as your money. Most people are not financially literate enough to manage their finances properly. As a result, they cannot retire early because they are not financially stable (Pan, 2019). This kind of financial knowledge that helps you to save for retirement is unfortunately not taught in schools and colleges. The best way to learn is through experience or if someone takes the time to teach you. In some cases, you may have to engage the services of a financial planner, which will be quite a process since you have to build a relationship with them.

Factor 4: Maintain Your Investments

Maintaining your investments entails building your asset base rather than accumulating short-term liabilities. People who try to enjoy life without understanding liabilities find themselves going into debt. Make it a point to always focus on those things that give you profits in the long term. A good investment is similar to planting a fruit tree. In the long run, it will yield fruits for you, focus on such investments and continue to build.

EXAMPLES OF TEENAGERS WHO ARE PLANNING FOR RETIREMENT

In this section, we will explore the stories of teenagers who have had a head start on their retirement savings. These teenagers are already planning for their later years. You could derive some motivation from them and get started with your own planning, too.

Eric Zhao

Eric Zhao is a teenager who decided to save so that he could have the security that his parents did not have. His parents were immigrants from China to the United States. Eric was born into a family that was not so well-to-do but had big dreams. Later on, the family opened their acupuncture clinics. Zhao has realized that without a strong financial foundation, life can be very scary. At the age of nine, he was hit by a car and was badly injured. Considering that there was no health insurance, the hospital bill was staggering. He realized the need to have a good financial plan, including health insurance. This has been his main drive to start saving now so that he will not have to worry about the well-being of his family in the future.

His parents have helped him to create a financial plan so that he doesn't have to graduate from college with a heavy student loan like his parents and sister. According to his plan, he saves 50% of everything that he earns and a substantial figure in his credit union savings account. He plans to open a retirement account and invest in stocks to ensure his financial life after retirement (Mitra, 2020).

Zach Sprung

Zach Sprung is just like any other typical teenager. He hangs out with his friends, plays hockey, and attends school. At the same time, he is saving for retirement. He is 17 years old, and he began investing $3,000 when he was 14. Having contributed three times, the value is now up to $11,000. Zach says he is sitting back and letting compound interest do the work for him.

Zach is a little bit ahead of most teens when it comes to comprehending the power of compound interest. His father, a certified financial planner, has contributed greatly to his son's financial literacy. Sprung helped out his father at his company over summers and in some cases, went for some hockey games to earn some extra cash. Zach's father wants him to understand the importance of saving for the future, and so for every dollar that Zach saves, his father matches it with spending money.

STEPS TO PLAN FOR RETIREMENT

Now that you understand the importance of having a retirement account, it is about time we explore the steps in planning for retirement. Having an idea of what you want your retirement to look like, and taking these steps will help you to make a wholesome and successful plan.

Understand the Different Types of Retirement Accounts

The easiest way to start saving for retirement if you are under 18 is to open a custodial IRA. Your parent or guardian opens this account for you, but the account will be in your name. The parent, however, retains control of the money in the account until you attain the legal adult age according to your state. When you open the IRA, it can either be a traditional or Roth IRA. Roth IRAs are considered to be the best for kids. The major advantage of Roth IRAs over traditional IRAs is that while traditional IRAs give you a tax break on the money you contribute, Roth IRAs give you a tax break on the money you take out. You are also able to withdraw the contributions made to a Roth IRA before you hit the age of 59, and you can withdraw half of it without incurring tax penalties. Other good accounts to consider are 401(k)s.

Open an Account

Having decided on which account you would prefer, the next step is to open the account. Usually, when you engage brokerages, they will advise you on what is needed for you to open an account, and the process should not be difficult.

Understand How Much Time You Have Before Retiring

Depending on your retirement plan, you only have so much time until you retire. This time frame is what you need to be sure about. When you know the number of years that you are going to contribute to your retirement account before the first payout, it helps you to figure out how many contributions you have to make before you can achieve your desired retirement amount.

Calculate Your Average Needs

Expenses like health care can be quite high in late life. Other costs, like clothing and transport, may be significantly reduced. Depending on how your life is structured after retirement, your spending will differ. Considering those things like medical costs, you may find that your future expenses will be much higher than they are now and, in some cases, much lower. This is why you need to sit down and try to determine your average needs in order to create a solid retirement plan.

Decide How Much You Need to Save Each Month

Having answered all the questions pertaining to retirement, it all boils down to how much you have to save every month to achieve what you have planned. The most important thing you should ensure is consistency. When you have determined how much you need to pay each month, you need to stick to it. Always be on the lookout for ways to increase your contribution so as to get the most out of your plan.

THE RETIREMENT CALCULATOR

Here is an example of what your retirement account would look like, given the following circumstances. If today you were to put $2,000 in a Roth IRA at an interest of 7%, and you do not touch it for 50 years, it will be $65,560 at the end of the 50 years. If you wait ten years from now to make the investment, it will amount to $32,622. Do you see the huge difference in earnings? Imagine what the outcome would be if you were to save $2,000 every year that you work. That would be a seven-figure income at the end of the horizon.

It is now clear that the best time to start investing is now. The longer you wait, the lower your income at your time of retirement. The best thing to do now is to choose a perfect retirement account, create a sound retirement plan that guarantees success, and then start working on it. If you are consistent in your plan and keep investing, you are likely to have a very secure future. Never make the mistake that most teens make, that is, waiting until later to start thinking about their future. Start now and experience the difference.

8

THE TEENAGE FINANCE GLOSSARY

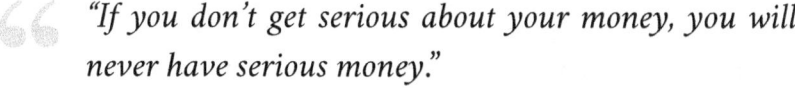 *"If you don't get serious about your money, you will never have serious money."*

— GRANT CARDONE

Knowing the financial terms is crucial to you as you build financial habits that will come in handy for a lifetime. Such knowledge makes it easier for you to grasp financial concepts and be able to move forward. The jargon in the financial world should be at your fingertips so that you will enjoy the journey of learning and managing finances. So, knowing the terminology and using the correct jargon can make you feel comfortable when dealing with complex issues that are related to money. You will also be able to ask the correct questions to bankers, financial advisors, or loan officers whenever you need clarity. For you not to be blindsided when entering the world of finance and money, this chapter will explore some of the frequently used terms that you can refer to.

THE FINANCE GLOSSARY FOR TEENS

This financial glossary is helpful to you as it covers the terms that you are more likely to come across as you explore the world of money. You will enjoy your journey of earning and saving money for the future. You may also feel at ease when you engage in conversations about finances, in addition to being able to contribute your views.

1. **401(k):** This is a retirement savings plan that is instituted by an employer for the employees. There will be an account where employees put a certain percentage of their salaries so that they can use it when they retire. This money will earn interest. You are assured of future income after retirement if your company has a 401(k) plan.
2. **Acquisition:** This is when a company buys all or more than 50 percent of the shares of another organization. This way, the acquirer may have control over the company and can make decisions without consulting other shareholders. In this case, the acquirer is regarded as the major shareholder.

3. **APR:** This is an abbreviation for "annual percentage rate." This term refers to the cost of borrowing money because it includes the interest and fees that are charged for you to be given a loan. The APR does not include compounding interest. It is expressed as a percentage and is paid yearly until the term expires. The APR can help you to compare banks in search of the one that offers the lowest rates on either loans or credit cards.
4. **APY:** The annual percentage yield (APY) is the actual rate of return that you gain on your investment in a year. The APY includes compound interest, and it is calculated periodically, thereby adding value to the balance. So, the more the investment is compounded often, the bigger the interest and total earnings. The APY is used on certificates of deposit, savings, and checking accounts. If you have a certificate of deposit, the highest APY is used to compensate for your sacrifices. This is because you are not allowed to use the funds in a CD, and a penalty is charged for withdrawals made during the agreed term.
5. **ATM:** An automated teller machine (ATM) is a self-service electronic banking outlet that can be found at bus or railway stations, restaurants, shopping centers, high-traffic areas, or even inside and outside the bank. You can withdraw, deposit, transfer money to another account, and pay bills at the ATM without the help of the teller. You can also access your money

using a debit or credit card. Withdrawals attract a fee that is charged by the bank that holds your account, the operator of the ATM that is from a different bank, or both. You may shoulder extra charges if you use your card in other countries. The ATM is convenient as it allows you to quickly perform transactions. The ATM is also referred to as an automated bank machine (ABM) or cash machine in other countries.

6. **Assets:** These are possessions that have economic value. Assets can be stocks, real estate, bonds, cash, or personal belongings like cars. Assets are grouped into current and fixed assets. Current assets like accounts receivables, prepayments, stocks, and cash equivalents can easily be turned into monetary values, and you are recommended to convert them within a year. Fixed assets are resources with a life expectancy that is more than one year, like machinery, buildings, and motor vehicles. Depreciation is calculated on fixed assets, and it indicates whether they are losing or gaining their earning power.

7. **Banker's check:** It is a check that is drawn by the bank from its funds on behalf of the client. The banker's check is signed by the cashier. This check is used when you want to buy items with greater value, like a house or car. The bank gives assurance to the seller that they will certainly get their money as there

is no way the check can bounce. So, for you to get the banker's check, go to your local bank. You should pay the amount equivalent to that on the check and also settle all the applicable fees to the teller. You will get the banker's check and present it to the seller as payment when purchasing an item.

8. **Bonds:** This is money you lend to the government, corporation, or municipality. The money will be used on projects. You can receive payback on bonds at a fixed rate and time. Variable rates can also be used on bonds. Loaning the government is less risky, although you do not own the entity. Your investment is secure because the state is unlikely to default on the repayment. The interest rate on bonds is lower, but you are assured of the returns on investment.

9. **Brokerage account:** This account permits you to sell or buy a wide range of investments like Exchange Traded Funds (ETFs), bonds, mutual funds, or stocks. You can use the money in the brokerage account however and whenever you feel like at the same time saving for your college tuition or retirement. So, you need this account before you start investing.

10. **Budget:** The plan on how you intend to use your money is called a budget. It can be described as the forecast of receipts and expenditures for a stipulated period, for example, a month or year. You can prepare a monthly budget for yourself so that you

manage your expenses and be ready for any mishap. A budget is essential as you can be able to buy big, expensive items without borrowing. It also helps you to keep an eye on your earnings and expenditures. Budgeting does not stop you from using your money the way you want. It simply helps you to assume more control over your money.

11. **Cash:** This refers to a currency in its physical form. The money can either be coins or notes. In the financial world, cash can include money in the bank account and marketable securities like government bonds.

12. **Certificate of deposit (CD):** This is a saving certificate issued by the bank when you deposit a certain amount of money for a fixed time. The bank will use your money for a specific period. The money will gain interest at a fixed rate. Your money will earn interest as long you do not violate the terms and conditions until the agreed time expires. This could be, say, over a period of one, two, or five years. You are not allowed to deposit or withdraw funds from the account before the term ends. You will be penalized if you withdraw the money earlier. The penalty is called the early withdrawal fee.

13. **Checking account:** This account allows you to pay bills, make deposits, and make withdrawals. The checking account should be at a bank and can be called a draft account if it is at a credit union. It is

also called a transactional account because you can access your money whenever you feel like using it. The checking account is mainly for day-to-day activities.

14. **Claim:** This is a request for compensation by the insured to an insurance company. A claim is made only for the covered losses. For you to be covered, your policy should be up to date. So, you should religiously pay your monthly premiums so that the insurer can pay you when the insured risk occurs.

15. **Compounding interest:** This is the interest you gain on top of both another interest and the principal amount. Compounding interest can be credited.

16. **Credit:** If you buy goods or services now and pay for them later, that is called credit. Your bank can offer you credit facilities in the form of credit cards. You can use the bank's money and make the repayment the following month. The bank pays expenses on your behalf but at an interest. If you fail to pay back the whole amount in one month, you can pay the agreed minimum value. You should make the repayment as soon as possible because the more you delay, the greater the value of the money that you owe, considering that the bank will continue charging interest on the amount unpaid balance. You should use a credit card only if you are capable of paying it back.

17. **Credit score**: This is a report that is formulated by the credit bureau indicating how you handle your finances. The credit score is represented by a three-digit number that ranges between 300 and 850. The higher scores show that you were paying your debts on time, and you automatically qualify for lower interest rates on loans. Lower scores show that you struggle with paying back your debts. Based on this, you may be denied loans in the future, or you may be charged higher interest rates.
18. **Debt:** This refers to the money that you owe someone. If you take a loan or use a credit card, you are in debt. You should pay your debts within the agreed period to avoid penalties.
19. **Debit:** When you debit your account, it means some funds have been subtracted, and the balance has been reduced. That's why the bank issue debit cards. You are only using the money in your account until it's finished, and no further than that.
20. **Direct deposit:** This is when you directly transfer money electronically from your account to the recipient. No paperwork is involved when making a direct deposit. The service is fast and convenient.
21. **Diversification:** This is when you spread the risk of loss among a wide variety of investments and savings options. The chances of failing on all your savings and investments are very low. If one fails, the other might excel. Diversification enables you not to put

all your money in one basket, thereby enabling you to spread the risk.
22. **Dividend:** This is the money that you receive when the company you invested in makes a profit. Shareholders are the ones who receive dividends usually at the end of each trading period, for example, at every year-end.
23. **Emergency fund:** This is money set aside for emergencies like sickness, or if you lose your job unexpectedly. Your emergency fund should cover your expenses like rent, transport, and food for at least three or six months. As a teenager, you can also have an emergency fund that is mainly for just-in-case spending.
24. **Finance:** It is the study, management, and creation of investments and money. Finance involves the use of investment, credit, debt, and securities to fund your current project while expecting to receive income flows in the future. Finance is divided into corporate, personal, and public finance. As a teenager, you are focusing mainly on personal finance like mortgage planning, retirement planning, savings, and insurance.
25. **Financial literacy:** This describes knowing and understanding money concepts like investing, debt, and saving with confidence. This can also lead to self-trust and general awareness of financial well-being. Financial literacy can help you to develop a

feeling of control over your money. It can also cause you to make decisions that can develop greater life satisfaction, in addition to creating the ability to navigate unexpected scenarios like losing a job. You can also understand how best you can simultaneously allocate your money toward many, different goals.

26. **Health insurance:** This is a policy whereby the insured pays monthly premiums, and the insurer covers all or part of your healthcare costs. Whether the insurer will pay for all costs or just a percentage will be agreed upon when signing the contract. Health insurance usually covers dental expenses, surgical, medical, prescribed drugs, and maternity bills. The money can be paid directly by the insurer to the service provider. It can as well be given directly to you as a way of reimbursing the expenses you incurred during treatments. Some employers pay for health insurance on behalf of their employees. They can pay the full amount or half and the employee another fifty percent.

27. **Income:** The money that you get in business after selling your goods and services is called income. Income can also be received or earned as commissions, dividends on investments, gifts, tax refunds, salaries or wages, or contracted pay.

28. **Income tax**: The state, federal, and localities charge income tax on earned money like wages,

commissions, and salaries. They also charge income tax on unearned money like dividends and interest. The tax is charged on both personal and business income. Please note that not all localities and states charge income tax.

29. **Inflation:** This describes a decline in the value of money, accompanied by increases in the cost of living or general prices. When the rate of inflation is high, you may need more money to buy the same products. This means that your money begins to buy less.
30. **Interest:** This is the additional money that you earn or pay when you lend to or borrow from someone. Interest is usually pegged as a percentage. For example, five percent interest is charged on every amount you borrow from the bank. So, if you borrow $100 today, the interest is $5, and the total repayment amount will be $105.
31. **Investment:** This is when you use your money to start a business or project so that it may increase in value.
32. **Liability:** This is the money that you or a company owes to someone or other organizations in the form of accounts payable, loans, bonds, and mortgages. Liabilities like income taxes and accounts payable are crucial for the day-to-day running of the business.
33. **Life insurance:** This is a policy that is purchased for a specific period like five or thirty years. The policy

will cover you until the specified period expires. The payout is done if you die within the agreed period. So, if you outlived the initial policy period, you should renew it, but the premiums may increase.

34. **Loan:** This is the money that you borrow from someone or financial institutions. A loan is paid back, and you will be charged interest. There are usually terms and conditions on loans. You will have to pay back the money within an agreed time frame. Financial institutions set repayment conditions. Usually, a loan is paid back in installments. For example, you will be paying a certain amount every month for a year or more, depending on the type of loan. There are long- and short-term loans. The repayment period for long-term loans is five years and above.

35. **Mobile banking:** This is when you use or access banking services through your mobile device. You can do transfers, pay bills, and check balances using your mobile devices. You need to install the application for your bank on your mobile gadget so that you can have access to your account.

36. **Mobile deposit:** This is a way of depositing checks into your account using a mobile device. You should take a picture of the check and send it to your mobile banking application. The bank will acquire all the details on the picture and affect the transaction so that the money will be deposited into your account.

Mobile deposit saves you on time and the cost of traveling as you do everything in the comfort of your home.

37. **Mortgage:** This is a loan that you acquire so that you can buy a house. The money you borrow can also be called a mortgage if you use the value of the already-owned home against the loan. Mortgage loans are usually repaid over a long period of time, like ten years or more.

38. **Routing number:** This is a nine-digit number that is used to identify your financial institution. It is there to differentiate the financial institutions so that it can be easy to transfer money to other banks. Withdrawing money at an ATM of a different brand is made necessary because financial institutions can be able to trace and get their money from the right bank. You can think of a routing number as an address for your financial institution, and it is used mainly on electronic transactions.

39. **Saving:** This means putting aside a certain amount of money so that you can use it in the future. For example, as a teenager, you can save some funds to buy a car or pay for your college education. When you become an adult, you can save for retirement, vacations, or some projects. A financial institution can offer you savings accounts where you will deposit the money for a stipulated time. So, you can

have your savings account now at any financial institution and get started.

40. **Savings account:** This is an account at your bank where you can deposit some money for future use. The money will earn interest. This account can be called a share saving account if it is at the credit union.

41. **Stocks:** This is a type of investment where you also become the part owner of the company which you buy shares from. You will be sharing ownership with other members who also have shares of the same organization, and together you are referred to as shareholders. So, when you buy stocks or shares, you are anticipating that the company will do well. If the entity makes a profit, you will receive dividends. If it becomes bankruptcy, you may lose everything as you are also the owner, and there will be a need to pay off debts first.

42. **Stop payment:** This is a request to your bank to stop a payment that has not cleared yet. Stop payment requests should be in writing for record-keeping purposes.

43. **Tax:** This is money charged to every individual by the government, either directly or indirectly. Taxes are charged on salaries, goods, and services. Tax is also charged on locally produced products and imports. The government uses these funds to

provide goods and services to its citizens. Taxes are a source of revenue for the state.

44. **Tax refund:** This is money owed to you as a taxpayer by the government. If the total tax is less than your total tax payments, that's when you receive a refund.
45. **Value investing:** It is an investment strategy whereby the investors buy stocks that are being sold for a lesser amount than their book value. Value investors do their research on stocks they think the market is underestimating so that they will make money when these companies increase in value.
46. **Venture capital:** It is a type of financing or private equity that is given to small entrepreneurs or startup companies by well-off investors. Financial institutions, investors, or investment banks give their money as venture capital to small businesses that they believe to have exceptional growth potential. Venture capital can be in the form of services like managerial expertise.
47. **Volatility:** This refers to the degree to which market prices move up and down. So, if you want to invest in any security, make sure you check its historical volatility to weigh the risk involved. Stocks with prices that fluctuate wildly, hitting new lows and highs, are considered to be highly volatile. The stock with low volatility is the one that maintains a more stable price. The highly volatile stock is riskier because there are high chances of failure and success.

48. **Wire transfer:** This describes the process of electronically transferring money using the network that is provided by banks and transfer services agencies around the globe. You should provide the name and account number of the recipient when you are sending money. No cash is included when doing a wire transfer and the transaction can be done between banks or from a financial institution to a non-bank service provider like Western Union.

There you have it! You have just acquired a fully-fledged guide on saving money and achieving healthy financial habits. So, you can now prepare for a happy future by making and managing your finances in the best way possible.

CONCLUSION

Knowledge is a great weapon if you want to make any major changes to your lifestyle. This is probably why it is said that knowledge is power. This book is an information reservoir that can help you to kickstart your journey to financial independence. While some may argue that we don't choose to be poor, I think that we do, though indirectly. Your level of financial literacy determines your future position in the world of money. This is one of the main reasons why learning about finances is of paramount importance—you secure a more comfortable space in the world of money. Basically, you learn about finances so that you become acquainted with vital aspects such as getting income, spending, saving, budgeting, and growing your money. If well-mastered, all these aspects lead to financial independence.

Saving is one of the most difficult aspects of managing money, even for adults. However, if you want to grow your money and achieve some financial goals, you should learn this skill. Saving teaches you financial discipline, which enables you to spend outside the boundaries of your savings account. Saving begins with good budgeting techniques. On your budget, always set aside some money for savings and use the rest according to your allocations.

Whether you have already started working or not, a day will certainly come when you will need to retire. When this time comes, you should have enough income to cater or your day-to-day living expenses. This means that you have to plan and save for your retirement years. The challenge that many people have is that they start thinking about these issues when they are just a few years (or even months) away from retiring. Starting to prepare for your retirement era now is doing a great favor to yourself because you won't be in much of a rush. Moreover, the longer timeframe between now and your retirement year allows you to accumulate more money so that you can live more comfortably after your retirement.

Have you opened your bank account yet? You certainly need one. If you are below the age of 18, you will need the assistance of your guardians to own a bank account. Even under the surveillance of your parents, you can still practice good financial etiquette and master it over the years. You can then manage one independently once you reach or surpass 18 years of age. Banks like Capital One Money, Copper, and

Chase First Banking are some of the best available banks where you can open an account as a teenager. Don't be scared to have your own credit or debit cards at your age. The earlier you start dealing with these things, the better.

The moment you try breaking off from depending on your parents for everything, you will enjoy the feeling that comes with such financial independence. That alone will be enough motivation to push you toward even lesser dependence. This is absolutely possible! Remember the story of Brandon Fleisher, how he tripled the $48,000 that his parents had given him to $147,000 in the space of two years. Fleisher was only 13 when he invested the money, and he has already cleared his path toward financial independence and so can you. You simply need to start thinking about it and then put your thoughts into action.

It is my desire that this book has triggered financial literacy and the thoughts of becoming financially independent. If you already had this in mind, I hope this book enlightened you on how you get started. With this book in your possession, become a financial expert at such a young age and live the independent dream!

If you found this book informative and insightful, please leave a review to help another teenager to benefit from this wealth of knowledge.

REFERENCES

Bareham, H. (2000, June 6). *How to apply for a credit card and get approved.* Bankrate. https://www.bankrate.com/finance/credit-cards/how-to-apply-for-a-credit-card/

Brennan, D. (2021, March 2). *Benefits of a teenager getting a job.* WebMD. https://www.webmd.com/parenting/benefits-of-a-teenager-getting-a-job

Brown, J. (2012, July 11). *The top 10 entrepreneur teenagers who made millions.* Addicted 2 Success. https://addicted2success.com/success-advice/the-top-10-entrepreneur-teenagers-who-made-millions/

CareerAddict Team. (2018, November 14). *The 9 most successful teen entrepreneurs in the world.* CareerAddict. https://www.careeraddict.com/teen-entrepreneurs

CFI Team. (2019). *Personal finance: Definition, overview, guide to financial planning.* Corporate Finance Institute. https://corporatefinanceinstitute.com/resources/knowledge/finance/personal-finance/

Davy (2022). *Wealth management and capital markets dublin.* Davy.ie. https://www.davy.ie/

DeNicola, L. (2007, November 9). *How to use a credit card to build credit.* Www.experian.com. https://www.experian.com/blogs/ask-experian/how-to-use-a-credit-card-to-build-credit/

DeMarco, J. (2021, December 9). *10 different types of credit cards.* Bankrate. https://www.bankrate.com/finance/credit-cards/different-types-of-credit-cards/

Employment and unemployment among youth summary. (2018). Bls.gov. https://www.bls.gov/news.release/youth.nr0.htm

Follow this step-by-step guide to learn to create your first budget. (n.d.). The Balance. https://www.thebalancemoney.com/create-your-first-budget-453625

Fontinelle, A. (2022, April 24). *The biggest financial hurdles young people face.* Investopedia. https://www.investopedia.com/financial-edge/0712/the-biggest-financial-hurdles-young-people-face.aspx

REFERENCES

Forbes, S. (2018). *Empowering you to make smart financial decisions.* SmartAsset. https://smartasset.com/

Great tips for getting your first part-time job. (n.d.). The Balance. https://www.thebalancemoney.com/tips-for-getting-your-first-part-time-job-2058650

Heard of the 70:20:10 budget rule? (n.d.). Suncorp. https://www.suncorp.com.au/learn-about/money-habits/how-to-budget-with-the-70-20-10-rule.html

High school job statistics [2021] (n.d.). Zippia. https://www.zippia.com/advice/high-school-job-statistics/

How to make money as a teenager: 25 lucrative ways. (2021, August 11). Clever Girl Finance. https://www.clevergirlfinance.com/blog/how-to-make-money-as-a-teenager/

Income: overview, gross/net, disposable/discretionary income. (n.d.). Corporate Finance Institute. https://corporatefinanceinstitute.com/resources/knowledge/finance/income/

Kapoor, N. (2019, October 9). *5 incredible teen entrepreneurs that are inspiring.* YourStory.com. https://yourstory.com/mystory/5-incredible-teen-entrepreneurs-that-are-inspiring/amp

Karr, A. (2022, September 19). *Why it's important to save money at an early age.* Mydoh. https://www.mydoh.ca/learn/money-101/money-basics/why-kids-and-teens-should-start-saving-money-early/

Kuepper, J. (2022, July 2). *Trading without market noise.* Investopedia. https://www.investopedia.com/articles/trading/06/marketnoise.asp

Lee, A. (2021, September 21). *How to teach needs vs wants for kids and teens.* Mydoh. https://www.mydoh.ca/learn/blog/education/how-to-teach-kids-teens-the-

Mills, A. (n.d.). *Teen financial toolkit: Wants versus needs.* Blog.cypruscu.com. https://blog.cypruscu.com/teen-financial-toolkit-wants-vs.-needs

Mint. (2021, March 29). *Budgeting for teens: 14 tips for growing your money young.* MintLife Blog. https://mint.intuit.com/blog/budgeting/budgeting-for-teens/

Morin, A. (2019). *The pros and cons of afterschool jobs for teens.* Verywell Family. https://www.verywellfamily.com/the-pros-and-cons-of-afterschool-jobs-for-teens-2610471

Nast, C. (2015, July 27). *6 reasons you need to put yourself on a budget.* Teen Vogue. https://www.teenvogue.com/story/why-you-need-a-budget-plan

Nath, J. (2020, December 1). *The 10 Benefits of Having a Job*. Jobscan. https://www.jobscan.co/blog/benefits-having-job/

Practice job interview questions for teens (n.d.). www.understood.org. https://www.understood.org/en/articles/job-interview-questions-to-practice-with-your-teen

Profiletree. (2018, September 28). *How to become a teenage millionaire: 15 success stories*. ProfileTree. https://profiletree.com/teenage-millionaire/

Resendiz, J. (2017, December 14). *Credit cards for teens: Best options and what you should Know*. ValuePenguin. https://www.valuepenguin.com/credit-cards-for-teens

Samuel, S. (2021, August 8). *5 credit card habits of the rich*. The Motley Fool. https://www.fool.com/the-ascent/credit-cards/articles/5-credit-card-habits-of-the-rich/

Sandler, J. (n.d.). *5 benefits of teen savings and checking accounts*. Rivermark Community Credit Union. https://www.rivermarkcu.org/youth/resources/benefits-of-teen-savings-checking

Sippl, Amy. (2021, September 16). *How to evaluate your teen's daily living skills*. Life Skills Advocate. https://lifeskillsadvocate.com/blog/how-to-evaluate-your-teens-daily-living-skills/

Smith, B. (n.d.). *Best banks available for teens results from investopedia*. Investopedia. https://www.investopedia.com/search?q=best+banks+available++for+teens

Swabb, C. (2022, May 20). *7 investing strategies to prepare for bear markets*. Schwab Brokerage. https://www.schwab.com/learn/story/7-investing-strategies-to-prepare-bear-markets

Teen budget worksheet printable. (2008, July 24). FamilyEducation. https://www.familyeducation.com/printables/parenting-tools-printables/teen-budget-worksheet

Teen self evaluation. (n.d.). Youth Employment Service. https://www.yesithaca.org/teen-self-evaluation.html

These 28 jobs are great for teens. (n.d.). Trade-Schools.net. https://www.trade-schools.net/articles/jobs-for-teenagers

21 best jobs for teens. (n.d.). Indeed Career Guide. https://www.indeed.com/career-advice/finding-a-job/best-jobs-for-teens

What are job skills and why do they matter? (n.d.). Coursera. https://www.coursera.org/articles/job-skills

Whyte, A. (2018, March 22). *The pros and cons of teenage jobs*. Evolve Treatment Centers. https://evolvetreatment.com/blog/pros-cons-teenage-jobs/

Your Money. (2013, October 25). *Why teens need personal finance lessons*. NDTV.com. https://www.ndtv.com/business/why-teens-need-personal-finance-lessons-370467

www.ingramcontent.com/pod-product-compliance
Lightning Source LLC
Chambersburg PA
CBHW052358220526
45465CB00003BB/1151